Nat is a comedian, cook, professional potty-mouth, musician,
mental health advocate and award-winning, bestselling author who
happens to hate writing his own bio so has to get his partner Jules to help.
(Thanks, Jules.)

Nat's platform has enabled him to hold up a tongue-in-cheek mirror
to antiquated cultural norms, to promote a little kindness and to have a
chat about his own battle with mental health. His comedy and cut-the-shit
tutorials have collected a dedicated audience of over 4.5 million,
thanks to his sweary delivery and underlying message of inclusivity
and looking after ourselves.

When he's not filming, cooking or purloining rosemary from a local
traffic island, Nat can often be found indulging his love of rock'n'roll
and comedy, playing in bands and stand-up rooms around Australia and
abroad. He is the author of three bestselling books: *Un-cook Yourself*,
Death to Jar Sauce and *Life: What Nat to Do*.

Un-cook Yourself and *Death to Jar Sauce* won the Booktopia Favourite
Australian Book Award in 2020 and 2021 respectively, with Nat donating
the winning proceeds each time to Beyond Blue. All three books have been
shortlisted at the Australian Book Industry Awards. Isn't that nice.

 @natswhatireckon
 @nats_what_i_reckon
 @natswhatireckon
 @natswhatireckon

NAT'S WHAT I RECKON

SMASH HITS

RECIPES

ILLUSTRATED BY
**GLENNO, BUNKWAA,
WARRICK McMILES
& ONNIE O'LEARY**

CONTENTS

Introduction: Hey Hey Champions . . . iv

Pantry Ammo . . . 2

Kitchen Shit I Use . . . 4

Who Tagged This Book? . . . 7

Knife to See You . . . 8

How to Slice Like a Champion . . . 9

Chopping . . . 11

THE MAIN SHOW

Chilli Con Can't Be Fucked Quesadillas . . . 14

Forgive Me for I Have Shins Osso Buco with Couscous and Yoghurt . . . 22

Me, Myself and Guinness Pie . . . 30

Straight to the Pool Room Rissoles . . . 48

End of Days Bolognese . . . 56

BBQ-rious Pork Ribs with Indoor Corn and
Rosemary Sweet Potato Fries . . . 66

The Creamy Mushroom, Bacon and White Wine Situation . . . 76

Pulled Pork Taco Night . . . 86

Pizza Party . . . 94

Pork 'Yeah' Belly . . . 116

Rice Rice Baby . . . 124

Self Pie-solation Shepherd's Pie . . . 134

Lamb Moussaka Therapy . . . 142

Shanks 4 Comin' Lamb Shanks with Mash . . . 154

Sacrificial Lamb Rack . . . 162

Crowd Goes Mild Curry . . . 172

Winner, Winner, Roast Chicken Dinner . . . 180

Chicken Parmy . . . 188

Bond Eye Chicken Burger (Hold the Sand) . . . 196

Honey Bastard Chicken . . . 204

The (Chicken) Wings of Love . . . 210

Surf and Turf Mie Goreng . . . 218

Ceviche on the Beach, eh? . . . 226

Fish Cakes . . . 236

Zero Fucks Mac 'n' Cheese . . . 246

Spinach, Ricotta and Better with Feta Pie . . . 252

Spicy Pants Shakshuka (Bush Doof Rescue) . . . 262

The Cure (pumpkin and sweet potato soup) . . . 270

Chilli, Pumpkin and Mushroom Rhys-otto . . . 280

Red Curry Sweet Potato Soup . . . 288

Vegenator 2: Judgement Tray Lasagne . . . 296

Gnocch-on or Fuck Off Chilli Tomato Gnocchi . . . 312

Gimme the Fritz . . . 320

Quarantine Sauce V2 . . . 330

SUPPORT ACTS

Roast Veggies Like a Bloody Champion . . . 340

Get Fucked Roast Potatoes . . . 356

Incidentally Vegan Street Coleslaw . . . 362

(Not Even Shit) Rad Salad . . . 368

Go Focaccia Yourself . . . 378

SWEET SURRENDER

Die, Shitty Frozen Apple Pie! . . . 386

Jim's Tirameezoo . . . 396

Gimme a Break Celebration Cake . . . 402

Wake and Don't Bake Orange and Lemon Cheesecake . . . 408

Frownie Reversal Orange Chocolate Brownie . . . 420

Pavlova the Patience Cake . . . 430

Index . . . 438

Acknowledgements . . . 443

HEY HEY CHAMPIONS

So legend face, check this:

You're a bloody champion of a cook whether you know it or not, and I can fucken prove it!

For those of you keen to cook some awesome tucker, think of this collection of recipes like kicking a ball between a set of goalposts EXCEPT you can't bloody miss 'cause there are no fucken goalposts to worry about – just good times, smash hits and sterling feeds you can serve up without doing yourself a stress.

So here's the set-up for this book: I have brought together all the recipes from my previous two cookbooks BUT WAIT . . . there's more! 'Yeah, good one Nat, you just glued your two other books together and called it something different, ya snake in the grass?' Not quite, friend. I have only gone and added a shitload more recipes, tips about knife skills and a load of opinionated carry-on about what I reckon you do and don't need in your kitchen. Just sayin' there's a fair bit more going on in this new book, so don't you worry, I'm not trying to pull a fast one on ya!

There have been a few requests to include some big hitters from my channel alongside my classics, like The Crowd Goes Mild Curry, Go Focaccia Yourself and Sacrificial Lamb Rack in all their illustrated glory, so that's happened.

I've designed this here cookbook to take all the pain-in-the-arse guesswork out of what the fuck you're gonna make next, all while adding some more info on what you're in for or whether it's gonna be cheap, a good call for a crowd of ya mates, or rad to make for the young champions of the household. There's a whole fucken month's worth of recipes here to help you navigate your daily dinner dilemma, show a loved one you have their back with a winning homecooked feed or even just to give yourself a well-deserved dose of self-care.

And while I'm at it, can I just say that I reckon it's about time I published a solid, hardback cookbook, don't ya agree? No more of this bendable spine nonsense, champion. At long last, I'm joining the grown-up part of the cookbook universe so you can enjoy an authoritative, weighted feel whenever you chuck it on the counter. I want it to have that thud-like quality reminiscent of an expensive European car door closing. Mmm, the sweet sound of excellence.

While this book may have more literal weight to it than my previous ones, don't let that alarm you, my friend. The weight comes not from the gatekeeping of 'told ya so' cooking information; quite the opposite. Cooking food should put a smile on your dial, not be something that gives you *Minority Report* stress levels and the urge to have a meltdown in the back shed and just give up on home cooking and order takeaway. I say no to that!

I wanna help take all that superfluous, fussy bullshit out of ya kitchen and replace it with a series of fist-in-the-air 'Yes, this is fucken sick!' moments.

Smash Hits Recipes has once again been illustrated into comic form by my amazingly talented mates Onnie O'Leary, Bunkwaa, Glenno and Warrick McMiles, so even if you don't end up cooking anything, you will still have a good time looking at all the pretty pictures.

Rightyo then, champion, let us collectively cook some most excellent feeds together and feel like the champions we are. And don't forget about the added flex of being the owner of a respectably durable hardcover cookbook.

Let's party.

PANTRY AMMO

Like a solid friend or pair of killer jeans, there are a few things in life that always have my back. In the kitchen we deserve that level of solidarity. It's fucken annoying when you wanna cook the thing from the cookbook but you don't have all the fucken things in ya cupboard – I get it. I like to keep a few faithful staples stocked in my pantry so I know I always have enough of the essentials to spice weasel a dish, or because I simply can't be bloody bothered going to the shop to get all the tiny but important ingredients to cook a feed for Jules and me.

I'll rattle off a trusty list of winning backups here that often save the day in my house.

1. SALTS (YEAH, MORE THAN ONE)

'Yeah, good one Nat, everyone has salt, ya dickhead.' Might sound obvious and yes I may still be a dickhead, but not all salts are created equal. It's not totally necessary to have several but I like to have some classic hits cheap table salt, cooking salt, rock salt, along with some flaked salt to finish a dish with. You don't need to have every single type, but having one for cooking and one for serving is a little bit very noice.

Table salt is your most common set-up and does it all, more or less; it's not too coarse and is cheap as all get-out.

I use it to salt water for this reason rather than for seasoning at the end of cooking, but it's fine to use at any stage.

Cooking salt is usually bloody cheap and typically comes in a bag. It is a little coarser so is best used only for adding to water and sauces, but not so much for finishing a dish otherwise you'll feel like you're eating fucken sand.

Rock salt goes in ya grinder and is cheapest when bought in bulk. It can be used for any and all of your salination needs.

Flaked salt is the fancy shit that is great to finish a dish with just before serving and to have on the kitchen table.

2. BLACK PEPPERCORNS . . .

. . . For reasons of a fairly obvious nature that usually involve it going in a grinder and then onto food. Avoid eating whole or doing what I did a few years ago and accidentally unscrewing the shit grinder and tipping the lot into the 6 litres of chilli you've been making all day. *tears*

3. SPICES & DRIED HERBS

This list can be as long or short as you like but the big hitters should get you out of trouble in most cooking situations and are great to turn veggie leftovers into proper meals. The ones that get used the most in my house are cumin, paprika, garam masala, ground cinnamon, ground nutmeg, turmeric, chilli powder, chilli flakes, dried thyme and dried rosemary. With this selection you can make a shitload of curry powders, Mexican dishes, sauces, roasts – the list goes on.

4. TOMATO PASTE & TINS OF TOMATOES

Whether whole, peeled, diced or crushed, tins of tomatoes last almost forever. If you have the available bucks to hand over, spending a few extra cents or a dollar can make dinner a little nicer, but it's certainly not a must. Tomato paste is such a common ingredient in so many dishes, so is a ripper to have lots of in ya pantry. I buy the smaller tins or tubes to avoid wasting it or risk it going bad in the fridge after opening.

5. WHITE & BROWN SUGAR

In addition to being a popular ingredient for baking, brown sugar comes in swinging when you need to sweeten up a sauce. It's a little more malty and subtle than white sugar. The old white death is great for baking and putting in ya Tetleys, Jim.

6. COCONUT MILK/CREAM

Both are great for curries and coconut involved dishes (unless you hate coconut, in which case don't buy it).

7. BEANS & LENTILS

Stock up on red kidney, black and pinto beans, chickpeas, and red and brown lentils simply because they're fucken cheap, all rule and are full of rad shit for ya guts. Dried beans are great and cheap too, but if you're not the soaking beans type then go for the tins.

8. STOCK

If you've made it yourself then that's fucken unreal. Though I am known for flipping my shit at jar sauce, store-bought stock I don't see in quite the same light. It gets people cooking interesting stuff and I dig that, unlike jar sauce, which is a fast track to dumping loveless boredom and mundanity onto actual food. Stock is a great tool to have on hand. Cartons of veggie, chicken or beef stock last a long time unopened. If you made your own stock you can freeze it so it'll last for a solid whack of time, too.

9. OILS & BUTTER

A little butter, extra virgin olive oil and vegetable oil will get you out of most situations. A little sesame oil is nice to have around as a dressing or for stir frying.

10. RICE & PASTA

I like to have a few types of each and, friend – this shit is cheap. When it comes to rice, white rice (either jasmine or medium/long grain) is great for most dishes that call for rice. For Indian style flavours I prefer basmati, and for risotto I like arborio or carnaroli. Arborio is the easiest to find and is available in cheaper brands. When it comes to pasta, all dried pasta rules and lasts in the pantry for ages. I love to look out for bronze cut/extruded shit, but that's because I'm fancy like that. It tends to carry sauce a little better, so that's my excuse. There are varying levels of quality with pasta and I have my faves. Like with tins of tomatoes, if you have the means to buy some slightly nicer stuff, I usually try to, but it's not a deal breaker.

11. SOY SAUCE, SWEET SOY & OYSTER SAUCE

Stir-fry gold.

12. PLAIN FLOUR

Does heaps of shit and costs very little. Get lots and make sure it's sealed tight so those fucken little shit moths don't get involved.

13. 100'S & 1000'S

Because I like to party.

This list could go for days. More or less all of this shit is cheap, you can buy most of it in bulk to save some bucks and stop you resorting to takeout as much.

Hope it helps, champion!

KITCHEN SHIT I USE

I have a few bits of kit in the kitchen that make cooking actually enjoyable and not a fucking flog. A handful of awesome tools can make a huge difference to whether you love or hate making a meal. Commercial cheffing shops often have cheaper shit sturdy enough to take a beating, so they're worth visiting if you have access to one near ya.

Here are my go-to pieces of equipment that save my arse in the kitchen time and time again:

1. A FUCKING SHARP KNIFE

The number one thing that makes life so much fucking easier, safer and adds such a huge amount of joy to your time in the kitchen is a sharp knife. You don't have to travel to the ends of the earth to find the perfect blade, nor do you need to sell your car to afford a decent one. The real name of the game is that it is sharp and you keep it sharp. A blunt knife does your head in while also being unsafe – surprisingly more than a sharp one, would you believe. Some are easier to sharpen than others. If you are looking for a good workhorse, spend a few bucks on a half-decent stainless or carbon steel chef's knife. If you decide to go for carbon steel, be warned that it takes a bit more effort to maintain – see page 8 for more info.

Also, hot tip: don't throw your good knives in the second drawer down with all the other stupid shit, as this kind of behaviour is what sends it in the express post to the capital of Bluntville, banging around in there. And don't put it in the dishwasher either . . . just don't.

2. KNIFE SHARPENING GEAR

There are a zillion things out there that do the trick, the best of course is a sharpening stone and a steel, but if you can't be fucked with all that nonsense, there are loads of easy-to-use sharpening wheels and devices on the market to help keep your bad bois nice and sharp. Another hot tip is that your local butcher usually has a knife sharpening service if you can't be fucked with all that buggering around.

3. FAT WOODEN CHOPPING BOARD

Before I say anything, let me say I think glass chopping boards straight up should be banned. The clanging, banging noise alone when using one makes my hair stand on end while I die inside waiting for the thing to fucken smash. I love a big, heavy wooden one so it doesn't slide around like a fucking dickhead and give you the Jiminy Crickets. You can throw a tea towel or non-slip mat underneath if it's skidding about. A solid investment well worth the money. Super thin chopping boards tend to fucken warp after a while so I like the thicker ones.

When it comes to cleaning it, don't soak a wooden board in water unless you want to be cutting shit on a misshaped

pain in the arse; a little warm water and soap and then stand to dry gets you out of trouble. Keeping it oiled with a little mineral oil stops the water soaking into the wood, too.

4. HALF-DECENT SET OF POTS AND PANS

I get away with using mostly a big frying pan or sauté pan with a lid, wok (remind me to buy one, pls), large stainless steel stockpot and a cast-iron casserole dish or Dutch oven. Again, you don't have to spend a ton on this shit, as long as it's durable and can handle a bit of a workout. If you live in a share house then good luck with Teflon. I use a mix of stainless steel and non-stick pots and pans, depending on what I'm cooking, but a good big non-stick frying pan is a reliable and simple-to-use piece of cookware that can make things a lot easier. Of course, don't use metal implements on the Teflon or you will scrape it off and end up eating it or killing the joyous non-stick sensation. Another no-no is heating up a Teflon pan too hot without shit cooking in it, as this can fuck up the non-stick surface and it's not amazing for the old lungs to breathe in either. A wok is also a ripper and a very versatile piece of kit that doesn't just have to be for cooking stir-fried food. I swear by the huge stockpot, too. If you can score one, it comes in very handy for a tonne of different dishes. The cast-iron pot isn't totally necessary but it is a nice thing to have at your disposal. They stay nice and hot when you're cooking so are great for not losing heat when adding cool ingredients – keep an eye out for sick cheap ones.

5. FOOD PROCESSOR/ DECENT BLENDER/ STICK BLENDER

The food processor or a decent blender that can do a similar thing will help make quick work of otherwise lengthy chopping and blending a whole bunch of stuff. The stick blender is a killer for soups, sauces and even mayonnaise. It also saves you having to ladle hot shit out of a pot and back in when making soup.

6. WHISK

Just have one, though.

7. ELECTRIC BEATER

Unless you're on the gains train, then I recommend using one for a lot of baking stuff. Whipping cream is a flog without it.

8. DECENT GRATER OR MICROPLANE

A Microplane is the one-stop shop for grating and zesting and also awesome for shaving the skin off your knuckles if you slip.

9. A BUNCH OF STAINLESS STEEL MIXING BOWLS

Get all the sizes, they are cheap and help heaps. If you're like me and have all your shit in bowls ready to rock before you kick off, these will have your back.

10. A MICROWAVE

Just kidding.

11. MEASURING JUGS, CUPS AND SPOONS

'Cause measuring.

12. BAKING TRAYS

A good flat one and a nice big deep one are the shit for most stuff. Stainless steel is pretty great if you can find reasonably priced gear.

13. KITCHEN SCALES

Such a huge win. You don't need to fork out your life savings for one. Just so rad for helping to take the guess work out of stuff.

14. MORTAR AND PESTLE

Not only does it make you look like a real foodie nerd, a mortar and pestle is great for smashing seeds and herbs to bits and creating flavours that are out of this world. If your pepper grinder is a fucken piece of shit like mine, then the mortar and pestle takes charge easily. It's fun to play around with spices in it – highly recommend.

These are my faves that I use the most. Of course there are bits and pieces like wooden spoons, tongs, ladles etc., but I would fucken be here all day announcing everything in my kitchen if I did. You certainly don't need to have all this shit to make all the stuff in this book happen, but it definitely helps make life a little easier in the kitchen at the end of the day, and feeling stoked with some solid gear is a nice feeling when you go to cook up some radness again.

WHO TAGGED THIS BOOK?

raises hand Me . . . it was me.

The reason I tagged all the recipes is to help you get a good idea of what you're in for when it comes to the level of commitment required, whether it's gonna be a good one to serve to young champions or vegetarians, to ease your stress or save some money etc.

CHEAP AF

Bang for your buck, cheap as fuck.

COMFORT FOOD

Will bloody fill you up while simultaneously embracing you with a dose of solid contentment.

FEED THE TEAM

Will serve at least six champions no problem.

IMPRESS THE JUDGES

Gee that looks like a bit of a flex on the plate there.

KIDDO FRIENDLY

Will likely keep the fussy kiddos happy.

LOW STRESS

Like something stressful, but the exact opposite.

QUICK STICKS

Low levels of mucking about ahead.

SIDE MISSION

Bit of a sidewinder / sidekick / sideswipe? Maybe not that last one? Anyway, it means this dish is a great . . . wait for it . . . . side.

WORTH THE EFFORT

Little bit more stuff involved in this one, but definitely worth what you put in.

VEGO

For vegetarian champions.

QUICK KNIFE FACT SHIT:

STAINLESS. These knives are a great affordable and no bullshit knife choice. Easy to manage and maintain, they are by default a harder steel so do tend to take a bit longer to sharpen, but as a result stay that way for longer.

CARBON STEEL. I use these in most of my vids. They are the fancy looking roughed-up type that develop a dirty patina. They are as hard as steel (lol) yet sharpen up quicker. They tend to rust very quickly, particularly if you cut any citrus shit with them or leave them resting on a stainless bench for too long. I fucken love carbon steel knives but they take some TLC and oiling after use to keep from rusting.

SERRATED KNIVES. Great for cutting shit like bread or a shoe in half. To be perfectly honest I have no fucken idea how the fuck you sharpen them. Lots of informercials sell them as 'never go blunt knives' because they usually seem sharper thanks to lots of little pointed teeth that grip the surface of the food, so they can get away with not being as sharp. They have their place.

CLEAVERS. Big, heavy and great for chopping soft bone, not as great for smaller work. They have a wider edge and heavier weight to them so need to be sharpened at a more raised angle. They are great for chopping tougher stuff your other knives will struggle to with the added bonus of saving you from bunging up your other thinner, smaller knives.

HOW TO SLICE LIKE A Champion

Lots of people ask me how I learned to slice so quickly in my videos. The truth is by practising and most likely wanting to act cool and impress my friends. My dad started it, to be fair; he used to flex this shit hard out when I was younger – he wouldn't even look at the food he was cutting and somehow not cut his fucken hand off. I found it totally hilarious and pretty cool.

The real trick is to start slow. There is no rush unless you're working in a professional kitchen or running out the door.

Let's use a classic chef's knife and half an onion as an example. Onion (or tomato) cut in half, flat side down on a steady wooden cutting board. The safest technique in my book for slicing shit is to tuck your fingers in and not have them pointing towards the blade, otherwise . . . yep, get the bandaids or the vicar. Using your thumb and four other fingers to steady the veg in an open pinching kinda shape over the

top rounded surface, place the tip of the knife on the bench and rest the flat side of the knife along your knuckles, being careful not to lift the blade higher than your knuckles as you move the knife up and down, or they will fucken end up in the dinner.

Push the tip of the blade into the chopping board and keep it there as you roll the knife in a rocking/circular motion like tucking a lever down and forwards. As you slice, use your thumb to brace the back of the veg to steady it and as the open pinch made by your thumb and fingers closes up, this is when to stop and readjust your set-up.

To guide the depth and position of each cut, press the flat side of the blade against your tucked knuckles back towards your thumb so that as you move across the surface of the veg, you can decide where and at what angle to slice into it. Be careful to keep your thumb behind your pinched fingertips at all times or you'll be making a trip to the first aid kit and I will feel shit that you hurt yourself.

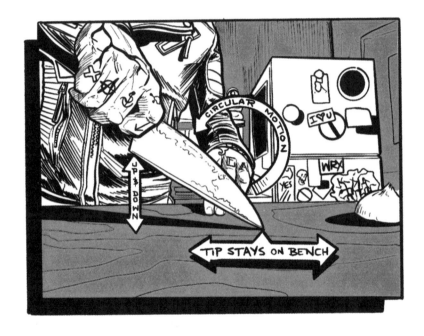

CHOPPING

This is a wonderfully noisy flex that lets everyone in the house know you're a bit passionate about cooking now. It is also a show pony danger zone so please take it easy. Microsurgery is no one's idea of a good time. Just ask Jules.

Chopping at pace comes with a high risk and is best with a sharp knife or you'll just be pointlessly tapping shallow lines into the fucken ingredients and likely needing to use more force and begin to increase the probability of fucking yourself up.

Let's use a carrot or zucchini this time (as long as you can be trusted not to put the zucchini in your fucken bolognese). Don't be scared to chop the veg or item into smaller parts to make the process easier. Same hand pinch shape as slicing

to brace the carrot, and your knife is flat along the knuckles again, but unlike slicing, instead you will lift the knife straight up and down as you travel your hand slowly backwards from the tip of the veg to the end.

Rather than push the veg with your thumb towards the blade, focus more on using the thumb to steady the veg and the curled tips of your fingers to act as a backboard for the knife to move across. Giving it a crack yourself and watching a few cool cats do it will get you chopping like a demon in no time.

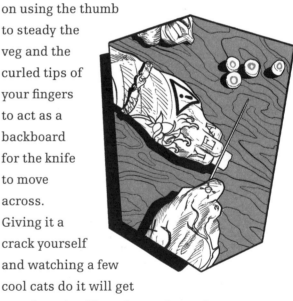

As always, do your thing at your own speed. Easy does it, practice makes perfect and all that nonsense.

Keep those knives sharp and a little patience and restraint by your side.

CHILLI CON CAN'T BE FUCKED QUESADILLAS

Maximum flavour, minimum time – gotta love that, eh?
It's pretty bloody quick and pretty bloody great to move
fast when you're super hungry, but you can also cook this
slow and low for as long as you like for a richer flavour.
Serve the chilli in a bowl on its own, with rice, or make it
into an awesome quesadilla – which I'm about to show ya.
To make it vego, the same amount of cooked lentils or
vegan mince works a treat. Follow the instructions on the
packet of plant-based mince for when to add it to the pan –
some need to be browned in oil to start with, while
others are added once the vegetables have softened. Omit
the chilli and dial down the spices if making for kids.

SERVES:
6
COOKING TIME:
under an hour

HECTOMETER: 4/10

KEY:
Kiddo Friendly | Feed the Team | Quick Sticks

INGREDIENTS

1 RED CAPSICUM
1 BROWN ONION, PEELED
1 BULB GARLIC, PEELED
1 HABANERO OR 2 BIRD'S EYE CHILLIES (OPTIONAL)
1 MEDIUM CARROT, PEELED
2 FRESH TOMATOES
APPROX. 600 G CHEDDAR CHEESE
OLIVE OIL
500 G BEEF MINCE
1½ TEASPOONS GROUND CUMIN
1½ TEASPOONS PAPRIKA
½ TEASPOON CAYENNE PEPPER (OPTIONAL)
140 G TOMATO PASTE
1 SMALL (100 G) TIN CHIPOTLES IN ADOBO SAUCE
2–4 CUPS BEEF STOCK
1 TIN (240 G DRAINED WEIGHT) PINTO/KIDNEY/BLACK BEANS
20–30 G DARK CHOCOLATE (OPTIONAL)
6 LARGE PLAIN WHEAT WRAPS OR TORTILLAS
BUNCH CORIANDER, ROUGHLY CHOPPED

GUACAMOLE

1 AVOCADO
½ RED ONION, PEELED AND DICED FINELY
HANDFUL FRESH CORIANDER LEAVES, ROUGHLY CHOPPED
1 CLOVE GARLIC, PEELED (OPTIONAL)
LEMON JUICE
SALT

SOUR CREAM,
FRESH CORIANDER LEAVES
AND HOT SAUCE,
TO SERVE

1 BOWL 1. CHOP YA CAPSICUM, ONION, GARLIC, ANY CHILLI YOU WANT TO INCLUDE, AND BANG IN A BOWL.

2 BOWL 2. SHRED THE CARROT ROUGHLY WITH A GRATER AND PLACE IN ITS OWN BOWL.

3 4 BOWLS 3 & 4. HALVE YOUR TOMATOES, SQUEEZE THE SEEDS OUT AND DICE, THEN PUT EACH ONE INTO ITS OWN BOWL. (WE'RE SAVING ONE FOR THE QUESADILLAS.)

5 BOWL 5. SHRED YA CHEESE.

GUACAMOLE

FOR THE GUACAMOLE, LITERALLY ALL YA HAVE TO DO IS SCOOP THE AVO OUT OF ITS SKIN INTO A BOWL, STIR THROUGH THE RED ONION AND THE CORIANDER (OPTIONALLY MINCE A GARLIC CLOVE INTO IT, TOO), ADD A SQUEEZE OF LEMON JUICE AND A PINCH OF SALT, AND MASH TOGETHER WITH A FORK. COVER AND SET ASIDE OR PUT IN THE FRIDGE FOR A SEC.

QUESADILLA

TIME TO MAKE YOURSELF A DANG QUESADILLA, NAPOLEON.

GET A COLD FRYING PAN WITH NO OIL AND PLACE IN A WRAP OR TORTILLA.

WE ARE GONNA SPOON INGREDIENTS OVER ONE HALF OF THE WRAP AND LEAVE THE OTHER OPEN TO FOLD OVER IN A LITTLE WHILE.

DON'T MAKE THE ROOKIE MISTAKE OF TRYING TO STACK TWO WRAPS ON TOP OF EACH OTHER AND FLIPPING THAT FUCKEN MASSIVE FLOPPY HEADACHE, AS YOU'LL LIKELY THROW A TONNE OF SHIT ALL OVER YOUR FUCKEN KITCHEN CEILING AND WONDER WHAT YOU HAVE DONE WITH YOUR LIFE.

ONE TORTILLA AT A TIME.

ORDER OF INGREDIENTS IS IMPORTANT, CHAMPION: YOU WANT IT TO STICK TOGETHER OR YOU'LL MAKE THE ABOVE HAPPEN. DON'T OVER FILL IT, EITHER, SINCE THIS WILL MAKE IT HARDER TO FLIP – THEY DON'T NEED TO BE FILLED RIGHT TO THE EDGE: LEAVE 1 CM EMPTY SO THE FILLING STAYS IN.

1ST STEP GOES TORTILLA WRAP INTO A COLD FRYING PAN.

2ND STEP GOES A SEMICIRCLE OF SHREDDED CHEESE IN A HALF-MOON SHAPE.

3RD GOES THE CHILLI MIXTURE ON TOP OF THE CHEESE.

4TH GOES A FEW PIECES OF UNCOOKED TOMATO FROM WHEN YOU DESEEDED AND DICED IT EARLIER.

5TH GOES A HANDFUL OF CORIANDER (OPTIONAL).

6TH TOP THE SHIT WITH ANOTHER SPRINKLING OF CHEESE. HAVING CHEESE IN CONTACT WITH BOTH HALVES OF THE TORTILLA WILL HELP TO STICK IT TOGETHER AND STOP IT FALLING APART.

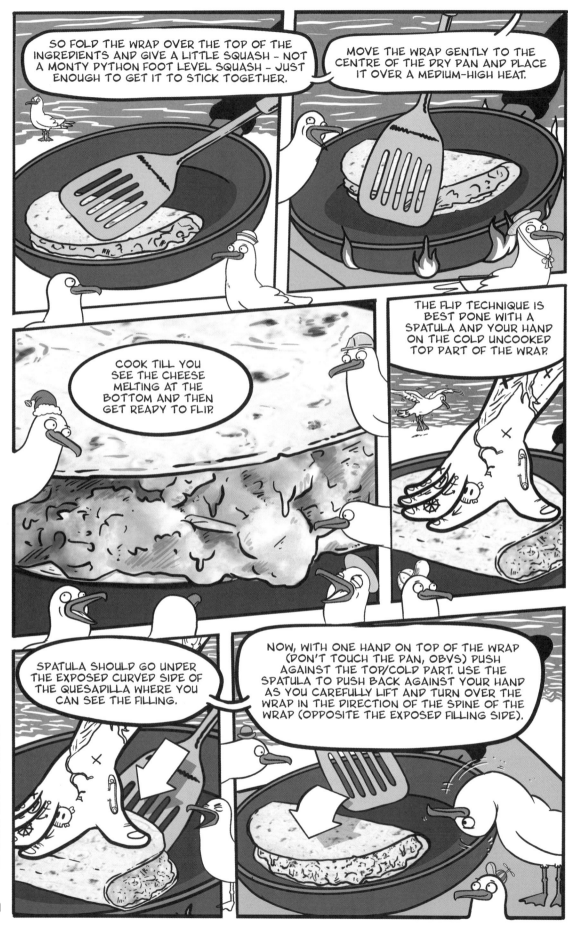

FORGIVE ME FOR I HAVE SHINS

(OSSO BUCO W. COUSCOUS & YOGHURT)

At a glance, osso buco is pretty fancy sounding shit.
In truth it's actually a really cheap cut of stewing meat
and would you believe it comes from the shin of the cow,
kinda like a lamb shank but bigger. It is very fucken easy
to cook. With a similar cooking vibe to lamb shanks,
osso buco falls apart in your mouth when cooked for
a couple of hours. Be your own fancy restaurant
at home without having to fork out the price of
leaving the house.

SERVES:
4
COOKING TIME:
2½–3 hours

HECTOMETER: 5/10

KEY:
Impress the Judges │ Worth the Effort

INGREDIENTS

3 TABLESPOONS PLAIN FLOUR
SALT & PEPPER
4 BEEF OR VEAL OSSO BUCO
2 RED ONIONS, PEELED
1 OR 2 ENTIRE GARLIC BULBS, PEELED
1 RED CAPSICUM, SEEDED AND ROUGHLY DICED
3 CELERY STALKS
4 DUTCH CARROTS OR 1 REGULAR CARROT, PEELED (DUTCH CARROTS ARE THE SMALL, BUGS BUNNY LOOKING CARROTS WITH THE SILLY GREEN SHIT STILL ON THEM)
1 OR 2 LONG RED CHILLIES - OR 1 HABANERO CHILLI IF YOU'RE FEELING TOUGH, SLICED (OPTIONAL)
1 OR 2 THUMBS OF GINGER, PEELED AND FINELY GRATED/MINCED
HALF A TIN (200 G DRAINED WEIGHT) CHICKPEAS
OLIVE OIL
1 TABLESPOON BUTTER
¼ TEASPOON NUTMEG
2 TEASPOONS GROUND CUMIN
1 TEASPOON TURMERIC
1 TEASPOON SMOKED PAPRIKA
1 TEASPOON ALLSPICE
1 TEASPOON CINNAMON
2/3 TEASPOON CAYENNE PEPPER (OPTIONAL)
250 ML HALF-DECENT RED WINE (CAB SAV OR PINOT WORK WELL, BUT ANY OLD SHIT WILL DO IN A PINCH)
3 TABLESPOONS TOMATO PASTE
1 × 400 G TIN WHOLE PEELED TOMATOES
3 BAY LEAVES
1 TABLESPOON BROWN SUGAR
3 CUPS BEEF STOCK
HANDFUL CHOPPED CORIANDER, TO SERVE
1 LEMON CUT INTO 4 WEDGES, TO SERVE

COUSCOUS (EASY AF)

200 G COUSCOUS
HALF HANDFUL CURRANTS OR SULTANAS (OPTIONAL)
220 ML HOT CHICKEN STOCK OR WATER
JUICE OF HALF A LEMON
HANDFUL CHOPPED CORIANDER OR PARSLEY
SALT

YOGHURT

1½-2 CUPS GREEK-STYLE OR PLAIN YOGHURT
SQUEEZE LEMON JUICE
½ TEASPOON GROUND CUMIN
½ TEASPOON GROUND CORIANDER

PREHEAT YOUR OVEN TO 170°C FAN-FORCED (190°C CONVENTIONAL). SIFT 3 TABLESPOONS PLAIN FLOUR ONTO A TRAY OR PLATE AND ADD A GOOD CRACK OF SALT AND PEPPER. DUST THE OSSO BUCO IN THE SEASONED FLOUR AND SET ASIDE.

FUCK THE REMAINING FLOUR OFF INTO THE BIN 'CAUSE YOU CAN'T USE THAT SHIT FOR ANYTHING ELSE NOW LOL.

DICE YOUR VEGGIES AND BUNG IN A BOWL TOGETHER - DON'T DICE THE FUCK OUT OF THE GARLIC, ROUGHLY SMASHED AND CHOPPED WILL DO. IF IT'S CUT TOO FINE IT WILL COOK TOO FAST AND TASTE LIKE FUCKEN SHIT.

GRATE GINGER INTO ITS OWN BOWL.

DRAIN CHICKPEAS, SET ASIDE.

GET A LARGE NON-STICK SAUCEPAN THAT HAS A LID, OR A CAST-IRON DUTCH OVEN TYPE OF POT, CRANKING OVER MEDIUM-HIGH HEAT AND BUNG IN A GOOD SPLASH OF OIL.

WHEN THE PAN IS HOT, SEND IT BRAH WITH THE OSSO BUCO AND BROWN OFF THE TOP AND BOTTOM. THE OSSO BUCO HAS A TENDENCY TO CURL UP IF YOU SEAR THE EDGES, WHICH DOESN'T MATTER BUT MIGHT PISS YOU OFF A BIT— I PERSONALLY DODGE IT AND JUST DO THE TOP AND BOTTOM FLAT SIDES. REMOVE FROM THE PAN AND SET ASIDE.

IN THE SAME SHIT-COVERED PAN, BUNG IN A TABLESPOON OF BUTTER AND THEN YOUR VEGGIES AND CHILLI AND FRY 'TILL STARTING TO LIGHTLY BROWN, MAYBE 5 MINUTES OR SO.

NOW TO DEGLAZE
(FANCY WORD FOR COOK THE SHIT ENCRUSTED ON THE PAN):
BUNG IN YOUR WINE AND SIMMER FOR A FEW MINUTES.
USE THIS TIME TO SCRAPE THE BURNT SHIT OFF THE PAN,
IF THERE IS ANY.
STIR IN YOUR TOMATO PASTE AND COOK FOR 1 MINUTE.
IN WITH THE TIN OF TOMATOES,
BAY LEAVES AND CHICKPEAS AND
STIR STIR STIR.
ADD BROWN SUGAR AND STOCK AND STIR TO COMBINE, BRING TO A GENTLE BOIL
NOW GENTLY BENTLEY
PLACE YOUR OSSO BUCO BACK INTO THE PAN,
SUBMERGING THEM AS BEST YOU CAN INTO THE SAUCE.
PLACE ON A LID AND BUNG IT IN THE OVEN FOR 2 HOURS.
FUCK OFF AND LEAVE IT ALONE FOR THE WHOLE TIME.
NO STIRRING OR FLIPPING NEEDED.

Me, Myself and Guinness Pie

There are few people on earth that love a pie more than Jules' dad, John. He takes this pie business very bloody seriously, and so he should. God knows we have all suffered many a shitty maggot bag from time to time, but if we are lucky enough we've also had the great fortune to experience a truly awesome pie that makes us reconsider all our previous servo dining moments.

When I discovered how fucking awesome it is to stew beef in Guinness, the words 'let's eat another pie' left my lips on multiple occasions, and I made a zillion of these fucken things until I got a heartburn so bad I just about burned down the house. Good news, though: I came good and now I'm ready to make the pie world proud with my own meaty frisbee full of all the flavour a mouth can hang with.

Let's eat like we mean it and not like we're filling up with E10.

SERVES:
6–8
COOKING TIME:
a few hours

HECTOMETER: 7/10

KEY:
Comfort Food | Feed the Team | Impress the Judges
Worth the Effort

INGREDIENTS

1.5 KG STEWING BEEF (CHUCK, BLADE, BRISKET)
2 TABLESPOONS OLIVE OIL OR VEGETABLE OIL, PLUS EXTRA IF NEEDED
1 LEEK
1 CARROT, PEELED
2 ONIONS, PEELED
ALL THE GARLIC IN THE WORLD (AT LEAST 1 WHOLE GARLIC BULB), PEELED
SALT & PEPPER
2 TABLESPOONS CHOPPED ROSEMARY LEAVES
2 BAY LEAVES
¼ CUP TOMATO PASTE
1 TABLESPOON BROWN SUGAR
440 ML CAN GUINNESS OR STOUT
2 CUPS BEEF STOCK
2 TABLESPOONS WORCESTERSHIRE SAUCE
¼ CUP PLAIN FLOUR
1 TABLESPOON BUTTER
2 SHEETS SHORTCRUST PASTRY
1 EGG, LIGHTLY BEATEN,
    FOR EGG WASH
2 SHEETS BUTTER-PUFF PASTRY

GEAR YA NEED

2-LITRE BAKING DISH

The Carbdashians

DON'T GO BACON MY HEA...

HELLS KITCHEN

Pudding up with it

NAT'S WHAT I RECKON
UN COOK YOUR SELF

A Real Pizza of Work

RUDE FOOD

Control your tempura

KALE ME, MAYBE

SPICE SPICE BABY

Y'ALL BREADY FOR THIS

THE BEST GUINNESS PIE EVER

INGREDIENTS

1.5 KG STEWING BEEF (CHUCK, BLADE, BRISKET)
2 TABLESPOONS OLIVE OIL OR VEGETABLE OIL, PLUS
EXTRA IF NEEDED
1 LEEK
1 CARROT, PEELED
2 ONIONS, PEELED
ALL THE GARLIC IN THE WORLD (AT LEAST 1 WHOLE
GARLIC BULB), PEELED
SALT & PEPPER
2 TABLESPOONS CHOPPED ROSEMARY LEAVES
2 BAY LEAVES
¼ CUP TOMATO PASTE
1 TABLESPOON BROWN SUGAR
440 ML CAN GUINNESS OR STOUT
2 CUPS BEEF STOCK
2 TABLESPOONS WORCESTERSHIRE SAUCE
¼ CUP PLAIN FLOUR
1 TABLESPOON BUTTER
2 SHEETS SHORTCRUST PASTRY
1 EGG, LIGHTLY BEATEN, FOR EGG WASH
2 SHEETS BUTTER-PUFF PASTRY

GEAR
2-LITRE BAKING DISH

KITCHEN

 SMASH HITS RECIPES

32

MAKE SURE THE PASTRY COMES UP THE SIDES OF THE BAKING DISH 'CAUSE WE WANNA JOIN IT TO THE LID SOON.

NOW BAKE THAT FUCKEN SHORTCRUST-ONLY DISH FOR 15 MINUTES TILL A LITTLE COOKED AND THEN REMOVE FROM THE OVEN.

FILL WITH THE RIGHTEOUS MEAT FILLING AND FLATTEN IT DOWN TO MAKE EVENLY SPREAD ACROSS THE DISH.

LAY OVER A PUFF PASTRY LID THIS TIME, CHAMPION, AND LIKE BEFORE DON'T GIVE YOURSELF TOO MUCH OF A HARD TIME ABOUT IT ALL BEING SUPER PERFECT. AS LONG AS IT'S CRIMPED OR SQUASHED TO THE SIDES OF THE SHORTCRUST SHIT TO CONNECT THE TWO PASTRIES,

THEN YA SWEET. BRUSH THE LID WITH MORE EGG WASH AND GENTLY STAB A COUPLE OF HOLES IN THE PASTRY TOP TO LET STEAM ESCAPE.

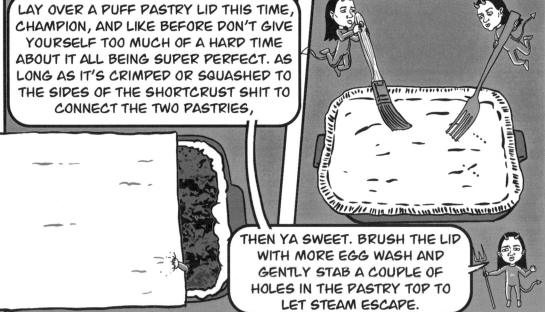

SMASH HITS RECIPES

INDEX

STRAIGHT TO THE POOL ROOM

B SIDE

100 50 0

NOISE REDUCTION

IN
OUT

RISSOLES

When rissoles were on the menu in the movie *The Castle*, I felt like I'd time travelled back to a kitchen table moment in the early 90s that quite a few of us have very likely enjoyed – fond memories always! I'll even take a burnt one these days if there's enough sauce on it. Rissoles are a great way to turn a regular burger patty into a feed that is a little more dynamic than just having a burger for tea. If you take the time to keep working the ingredients into each other in the mixing bowl, then you will no doubt end up avoiding the common complaint of 'my fucken rissoles always fall apart'. Buckle up for a real old-school Aussie classic here, and a bloody good one, too.

SERVES:
4–6
COOKING TIME:
under an hour

HECTOMETER: 3/10

KEY:
Cheap AF | Kiddo Friendly | Quick Sticks

PLONK!

INTO THE RISSOLE BOWL GOES THE RISSOLE MEAT. THEN GRATE IN YOUR CARROT, ZUCCHINI AND ONION. YOU CAN DO IT WITHOUT PUTTING YOUR BACK INTO IT, MR OLYMPIA. GENTLE PRESSURE WILL GET YOU THERE; IF WE WANTED IT THICK CUT, WE WOULD JUST DO THAT.

GET YOURSELF A BIG PINCH OF PARZZZLEY AND CHOP IT FINELY. CHUCK THAT INTO THE BOWL AS WELL, WITH YOUR GARLIC POWDER, ONION POWDER AND DRIED THYME. CRACK IN THE EGG AND ADD THE BREADCRUMBS, DIJON MUSTARD, WORCESTERSHIRE SAUCE, A BIG PINCH OF SALT AND PEPPER TO TASTE.

MR OLYMPIA

GRAB A LITTLE HANDFUL OF RISSOLE MIX AND GET SQUISHING. IT DOESN'T HURT TO SPEND SOME TIME HERE TO GET IT IN SHAPE, WORK THE AIR OUT OF IT AND KEEP ROTATING AND SQUISHING IT TILL IT LOOKS FUCKEN STUCK TOGETHER. GIVE IT A GOOD PUSH AND SQUISH IT INTO THE KIND OF RISSOLE SHAPE THAT YOU LIKE. CONTINUE MAKING RISSOLES OF YOUR PREFERRED SIZE WITH THE REST OF THE MIXTURE. I USUALLY GET ABOUT 8 OUT OF MY RISSOLE BOWL.

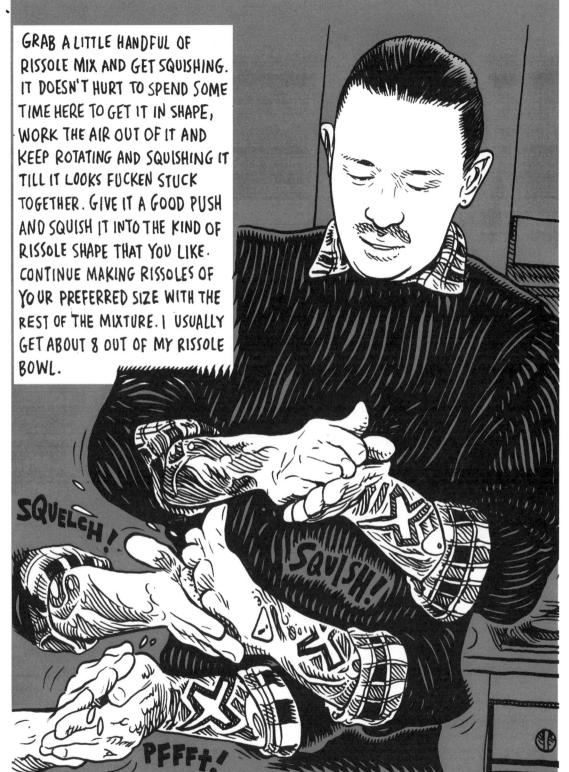

SQUELCH!

SQUISH!

PFFFt!

HEAT SOME OLIVE OIL IN A FRYING PAN TO MEDIUM-HIGH HEAT. LAY YOUR RISSOLES IN CAREFULLY AND COOK FOR A FEW MINUTES EACH SIDE OR UNTIL THEY ARE DONE. WATCH THE HEAT, HADES, AS TOO HOT AND THEY WILL LOOK LIKE A CUPPLA BRIDGESTONE TYRES.

IT'S A FUCKEN ALL-TIME BELTER THIS ONE. YOU CAN ADD AND REMOVE LOADS OF COOL SHIT IN RISSOLES SO GO EXPERIMENT IN YA LAB AFTER YOU'VE TRIED THESE. SERVE IT WITH SOME CLASSIC SIDES LIKE MASH AND ROASTED CARROTS, AND DON'T BE SCARED OF HAMMERING IT WITH YA FAV TOMATO OR BBQ SAUCE.

END OF DAYS BOLOGNESE

A
C-60

STEREO

This dish is one of the most classic hits of all time.
It can also be a classic bastardised punish if it's jammed with
a tonne of stupid shit. God knows the signature bolognese
recipe additions I've seen before have been nothing short of
fucking bizarre, I've even made a few strange moves myself
in the past – everything from barbecue sauce to Vegemite.
Now, by all means, put whatever you want in your sauce, but
the title of 'bolognese' loses its identity fast when ingredients
like zucchini and capsicum enter the room. Made my way –
I promise you a classic done right – it's like a good dance
move you can rely on without landing on your arse in
front of everyone.

SERVES:
6–8*
COOKING TIME:
under an hour
* depending on how sauce heavy you go

HECTOMETER: 4/10

KEY:
Feed the Team | Kiddo Friendly | Low Stress

INGREDIENTS

- 1 ONION
- 2 CARROTS
- 2 STICKS CELERY
- 150-200g PANCETTA (CAN SUBSTITUTE BACON)
- 25-30g BUTTER
- OLIVE OIL
- A BIT OVER 500g EACH OF PORK AND BEEF MINCE
- FRESH ROSEMARY, THYME OR OTHER SAVOURY HERB (OPTIONAL)

- GLASS OR 2 OF WINE (RED OR WHITE)
- 300g TOMATO PASTE
- 1 CUP MILK
- 1-2 CUPS CHICKEN STOCK
- SALT & PEPPER TO TASTE
- BAY LEAVES (WHO KNOWS IF THEY REALLY DO ANYTHING ANYWAY, SO LET'S PLAY IT SAFE AT 2-3)

- 500-750g PASTA (BUY SOME FUCKEN NICE BRONZE-EXTRUDED SHIT WOULD YA, THE COUPLE OF EXTRA BUCKS GOES A LONG WAY)

- PARMESAN, TO SERVE

HERE'S WHERE YOU CAN CHOOSE TO ADD SOME ROSEMARY. IF YOU LIKE, GO OUT AND PICK SOME, IT GROWS FUCKEN EVERYWHERE! JUST CHUCK IN THE WHOLE SPRIG, INCLUDING THE STALK. IF YOU PREFER TO USE ALTERNATIVE HERBS, GO FOR GOLD!

KEEP COOKING THE LIQUID OUT UNTIL THE MEAT MIX IS FRYING. ONCE THE LIQUID IS FRIED OFF ADD A GLASS OR TWO OF WINE.

THERE IS AN ARGUMENT THAT YOU SHOULD USE WHITE WINE OVER RED WINE BUT I'M NOT GETTING INVOLVED IN THAT ARGUMENT.

AGAIN, WITH THE QUALITY OF THE BOOZE, THAT'S UP TO YOUSE.

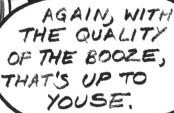

LET THE BOOZE COOK OFF FOR A COUPLA MINUTES THEN DROP IN YOUR TOMATO PASTE.

SEASON WITH SALT AND PEPPER, ADD THE BAY LEAVES.

I'M STILL CONVINCED BAY LEAVES ONLY GO IN FOOD TO MAKE IT LOOK LIKE YOU KNOW WHAT YOU'RE DOING.

THEN TURN THE HEAT DOWN

PUT THE LID ON

AND COOK IT FOR AS LONG AS YA FUUUUUCCCKKEEN LIKE.

GIVE IT AN OCCASIONAL STIR, AND IF IT STARTS TO LOOK DRY...

ADD A BIT MORE BLOODY STOCK.

YUMMO!

STOCK

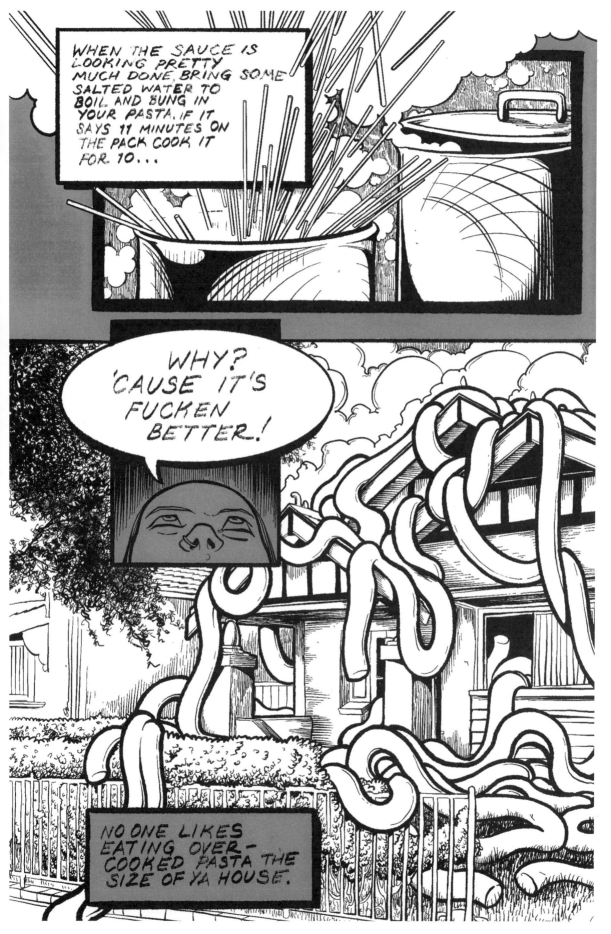

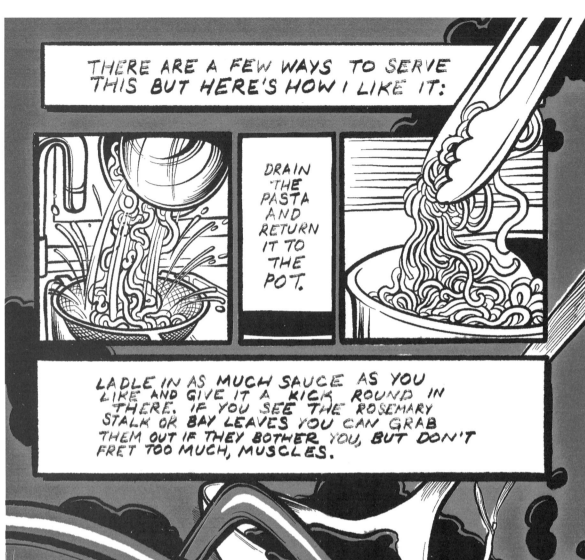

THERE ARE A FEW WAYS TO SERVE THIS BUT HERE'S HOW I LIKE IT:

DRAIN THE PASTA AND RETURN IT TO THE POT.

LADLE IN AS MUCH SAUCE AS YOU LIKE AND GIVE IT A KICK ROUND IN THERE. IF YOU SEE THE ROSEMARY STALK OR BAY LEAVES YOU CAN GRAB THEM OUT IF THEY BOTHER YOU, BUT DON'T FRET TOO MUCH, MUSCLES.

BBQ-rious PORK RiBS
W. INDOOR CORN & SWEET POTATO FRIES

So, you live in an apartment without a barbie, yet you longingly watch aggressive amounts of competitive *BBQ Pit Master*-style shows and wish you could join in. Well, don't let your lack of suitable equipment stop you, champion! You can still achieve that big BBQ energy without losing your rental bond by introducing an outdoor cooker to your lounge room and smoking the place out. I have a sweet-as BBQ hack called an oven that means you can still hang with the BBQ lords of the dance – and you probably have one, too. Ribs, believe it or not, are a solid winner in the oven. Don't let the gatekeepers of the ribo-verse tell you ya can't make awesome ribs without a BBQ, because you can.

PS. If you like a full rack per person, double the rub ingredients; the amount of BBQ sauce should be plenty to make all that lot happen, though.

SERVES:
4 (with half rack)
COOKING TIME:
3½ hours

HECTOMETER: 5/10

KEY:
Comfort Food | Kiddo Friendly

INGREDIENTS

1.3–1.5 KG AMERICAN-STYLE PORK RIBS (APPROX. 350–400 G PER PERSON OR DOUBLE THE WEIGHT FOR FULL RACK)

SALT AND PEPPER

RUB

3 TABLESPOONS BROWN SUGAR
2 TEASPOONS GARLIC POWDER
1 TEASPOON CUMIN
1 TEASPOON SMOKED PAPRIKA
1 TEASPOON MUSTARD POWDER
½ TEASPOON CINNAMON
1–2 TABLESPOONS OLIVE OIL

BBQ SAUCE

30–40 G BUTTER
1 MEDIUM BROWN ONION, PEELED AND FINELY DICED
4 GARLIC CLOVES, PEELED AND DICED
⅓ TEASPOON SMOKED PAPRIKA
20 ML BALSAMIC VINEGAR
1 HEAPED TABLESPOON MOLASSES (CAN SUB IN 2 TABLESPOONS BROWN SUGAR; MOLASSES IS BETTER, THOUGH ;))
1 CUP KETCHUP
1½ TABLESPOONS DIJON MUSTARD
2 TABLESPOONS WORCESTERSHIRE SAUCE

REST OF THE SHIT

2 MEDIUM-LARGE SWEET POTATOES 750G–1KG
LIGHT DUSTING OF CORN STARCH/PLAIN FLOUR
2 TABLESPOONS OLIVE OIL
ROCK SALT
BIG PINCH FRESH OR DRIED ROSEMARY
4 CORN COBS, HUSKS REMOVED
2 TABLESPOONS BUTTER
HANDFUL OF CHOPPED PARSLEY (OPTIONAL)

GEAR

FOIL – LARGE OVENPROOF DISH
RACK – BAKING PAPER
2 LARGE BAKING TRAYS

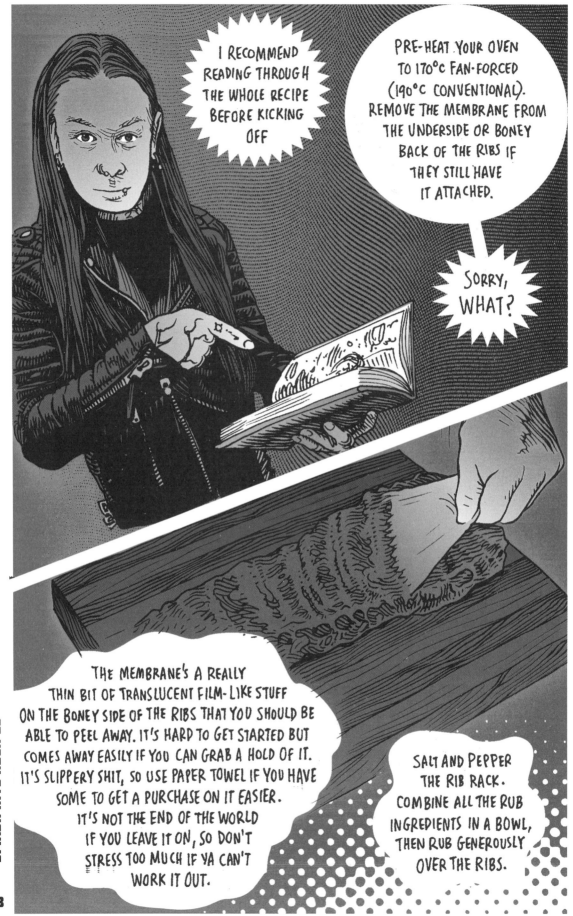

PSA: YOUR HANDS WILL BE COVERED IN TASTY YET DANGEROUS SHIT, SO CLEAN THOSE BAD BOIS AND **DO NOT** GIVE YOUR DIGITS A FLAVOUR-CHECK TASTE UNLESS YOU FANCY SPENDING THE REST OF THE WEEK ON THE TOILET BEGGING FOR UNCOOKED PORK BACTERIA MERCY.

WRAP THE RIBS TIGHTLY (AIR TIGHT) IN FOIL AND PLACE ON A RACK RESTING OVER AN OVENPROOF DISH.
TIP 1-2 CM OF WATER INTO THE DISH BENEATH THE RACK OR ALTERNATIVELY, IF YOU DON'T HAVE A RACK AND ARE JUST PLACING THE MEAT IN A DISH, POUR SOME WATER INTO A SECOND DISH AND PLACE IT IN THE OVEN SHELF BELOW THE RIBS.

**THIS MAY SEEM A BIT EXTRA, BUT THE WATER GENTLY STEAMING AWAY DURING THE COOKING TIME WILL KEEP THE OVEN ENVIRONMENT HUMID. IT'S JUST AN EXTRA STEP TO HELP STOP THE RIBS FROM BECOMING DRY TRASH.

IF THE WATER LEVEL GETS LOW, FEEL FREE TO ADD A SPLASH TO IT AS TIME GOES – NOT A HUGE STRESS.

GET YOUR PHONE TIMER READY, FREDDY. BAKE IN THE OVEN FOR 2·5 HOURS.

NOW TO MAKE THE BBQ SAUCE.
THERE ARE A FEW WAYS TO MAKE BBQ SAUCE. THIS IS A SUPER EASY WAY TO MAKE A KILLER ONE. YOU CAN KEEP THE LEFTOVERS IN THE FRIDGE FOR A WEEK OR SO AFTERWARDS IF YOU HAVE ANY LEFT.

IN A SMALL POT OVER MEDIUM-LOW HEAT, MELT THE BUTTER AND NICE AND SLOWLY SAUTÉ THE ONIONS FOR 5 MINUTES, BEING CAREFUL NOT TO BURN THEM OR THE BUTTER. LOW AND SLOW IS YOUR BEST MATE.

ADD YOUR DICED GARLIC AND KEEP COOKING NICE AND SLOW UNTIL THE GARLIC HAS SOFTENED AND THE ONIONS ARE TRANSLUCENT, STIRRING FREQUENTLY BUT NOT CONSTANTLY.

COOK THIS TILL IT JUST STARTS TO GET THAT LIGHT BROWN COLOUR TO IT. ADD YOUR PAPRIKA TO THE ONIONS AND GARLIC AND FRY OFF FOR 2 MINUTES.

THEN INTO THE ONIONS WITH THE BALSAMIC AND MOLASSES, COOK THIS TOGETHER FOR A FURTHER 3 MINUTES ON A SLIGHTLY INCREASED HEAT (MEDIUM).

FANG THE KETCHUP, DIJON AND WORCESTERSHIRE IN, STIR TO COMBINE AND COOK ON LOW FOR 5 MINUTES, ADDING A SPLASH OF WATER OR TWO TO THIN IT OUT A LITTLE.

GOD DAMN IT JACK!

WITH A STICK BLENDER, GIVE IT ALL A GOOD BLEND OR ALTERNATIVELY YOU CAN BUNG IT IN A BLENDER OR PROCESSOR THAT CAN HANDLE HOT SHIT BUT BE CAREFUL: HOT SHIT IN CERTAIN BLENDERS HAS A TENDENCY TO GO KABOOM AND FUCK UP YOUR KITCHEN AND AWESOME NEW SHIRT (SIMILAR TO MICROWAVING A GLOW STICK... DON'T DO IT), SO LET IT COOL A LITTLE BEFOREHAND.

THE
CREAMY MUSHROOM, BACON
& WHITE WINE SITUATION

For all those people who think carbonara
has cream in it, you're fucking wrong, champ.
This is the dish you're thinking of. Certainly no
one's idea of a health kick – but *goddamn* does it
make you feel good when you eat it.
What a bloody ripper.

SERVES:
4–5
COOKING TIME:
45-ish mins

HECTOMETER: 3/10

KEY:
Comfort Food | Quick Sticks

INGREDIENTS

1 BROWN ONION
250G BACON
WHOLE GARLIC BULB ⟵ PEELED
8 SPRING ONIONS
500G MUSHROOMS
1 TABLESPOON BUTTER
1½ TABLESPOONS PLAIN FLOUR
1½ CUPS WHITE WINE
500G PASTA
½ CUP CHICKEN STOCK
¾ CUP PURE CREAM
SALT
PEPPER
PARMESAN ⟶ TO SERVE
HANDFUL OF PARSLEY
⤷ CHOPPED
⤷ TO CHUCK ON TOP

STOCK
MADE FROM
REAL STOCK!

Pure
CREA

SIFT OVER YOUR FLOUR, STIR TOGETHER & COOK THAT OFF FOR A COUPLE OF MINUTES
THEN CRANK IN YOUR WINE AND COOK THAT OFF FOR 5 MINUTES.
RIPPER TIME TO ADD THE PASTA TO THE BOILING WATER.
COOK THE PASTA ACCORDING TO THE PACKET INSTRUCTIONS.

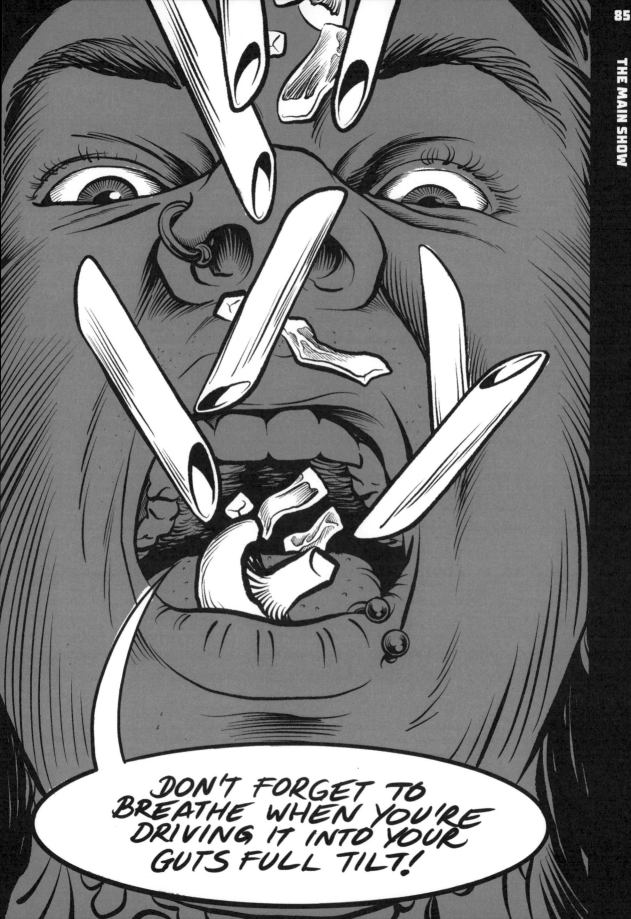

PULLED PORK TACO NIGHT

Taco night was always a very bloody exciting time for me as a kid. As a young fella, being able to choose my own adventure while filling a shitty, flimsy corn chip–style taco shell with sachet-seasoned mince and all the fucken cheese on earth was a truly bloody wild time. I've put away a lot of traditional Mexican food in my adult years, while living overseas, and omg it's fucken amazing stuff. The shit I've had from those fucken powdered flavour sachets here in Australia couldn't be further from those rad memories if they tried.

Why don't we try to channel the ravenous creativity and joy of being a kid at taco night, while also attempting to harness the obsessive gastropub pulled pork energy from the last ten years, and create something that gives us a way more righteous taco night and give sachet trash the bird.

SERVES:
4–6
COOKING TIME:
about 3 hours

HECTOMETER: 5/10

KEY:
Feed the Team │ Impress the Judges

INGREDIENTS

- 1.2–1.5 KG BONELESS PORK SHOULDER MEAT (SKIN REMOVED)
- 1 BROWN ONION
- 1 BUNCH CORIANDER, STALKS CHOPPED, LEAVES RESERVED FOR TACOS AND GUAC
- WHOLE GARLIC BULB
- 2 TABLESPOONS OLIVE OIL OR VEGETABLE OIL
- SALT
- 2 TEASPOONS CHIPOTLE POWDER
- 2 TEASPOONS SMOKED SWEET PAPRIKA
- 2 TEASPOONS GROUND CORIANDER
- 1 TEASPOON GROUND CUMIN
- 1 TABLESPOON BROWN SUGAR
- 2 TABLESPOONS TOMATO PASTE
- 400 G CAN WHOLE TOMATOES
- 2 CUPS CHICKEN STOCK
- 400 G CAN BLACK OR PINTO BEANS, RINSED AND DRAINED
- SOFT AND (IF YOU LIKE) HARD SHELL TACOS, SOUR CREAM AND SHREDDED CHEDDAR, TO SERVE

GUACAMOLE

- 2 AVOCADOS
- 1/2 RED ONION, PEELED AND FINELY CHOPPED
- 1 JALAPEÑO PEPPER, DESEEDED AND DICED
- 1 TOMATO, DESEEDED AND DICED
- HANDFUL CHOPPED CORIANDER LEAVES
- JUICE OF 1 LIME
- SALT

(OPTIONAL) QUICK PICKLE

- 1 JALAPEÑO PEPPER, DESEEDED AND FINELY CHOPPED
- 4 BABY CUCUMBERS, SLICED
- 200 G CHERRY TOMATOES, QUARTERED
- 1/2 CUP APPLE CIDER VINEGAR OR WHITE WINE VINEGAR
- 1/2 RED ONION, PEELED AND THINLY SLICED
- PINCH OF SUGAR AND SALT

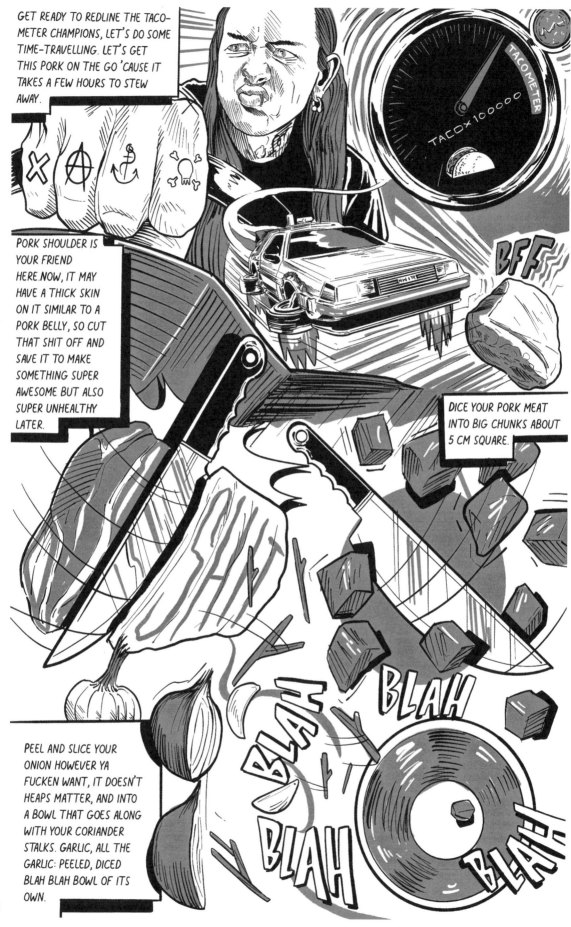

GET READY TO REDLINE THE TACO-METER CHAMPIONS, LET'S DO SOME TIME-TRAVELLING. LET'S GET THIS PORK ON THE GO 'CAUSE IT TAKES A FEW HOURS TO STEW AWAY.

PORK SHOULDER IS YOUR FRIEND HERE. NOW, IT MAY HAVE A THICK SKIN ON IT SIMILAR TO A PORK BELLY, SO CUT THAT SHIT OFF AND SAVE IT TO MAKE SOMETHING SUPER AWESOME BUT ALSO SUPER UNHEALTHY LATER.

DICE YOUR PORK MEAT INTO BIG CHUNKS ABOUT 5 CM SQUARE.

PEEL AND SLICE YOUR ONION HOWEVER YA FUCKEN WANT, IT DOESN'T HEAPS MATTER, AND INTO A BOWL THAT GOES ALONG WITH YOUR CORIANDER STALKS. GARLIC, ALL THE GARLIC: PEELED, DICED BLAH BLAH BOWL OF ITS OWN.

INTO AN OVENPROOF CASSEROLE THAT HAS A LID GOES THE OIL THAT YOU NEED TO HEAT OVER MEDIUM-HIGH.

SEASON YOUR PORK WITH ENOUGH SALT TO LIGHTLY COVER IT AND 'SEND IT' INTO THAT HOT PAN TO BROWN OFF FOR A FEW MINUTES SO ALL SIDES ARE SEALED. NOW TAKE IT OUT OF THE PAN AND TRANSFER TO A PLATE.

ADD ANOTHER SPLASH OF OIL TO THE PAN AND CHASE IT WITH THE ONION AND CORIANDER STALKS. 3-4 MINUTES LATER IN GOES THE FUCK-TONNE OF GARLIC, AND COOK FOR ANOTHER COUPLE OF MINUTES UNTIL IT'S SOFTENED.

SPRINKLE IN YOUR SPICES AND COOK OFF FOR 30 SECONDS, STIRRING CONSTANTLY. FANG IN THE TOMATOES, TOMATO PASTE AND STOCK AND BRING ALL THAT SICK SHIT TO A SIMMER, SIMON.

ONCE ALL THAT IS AS IT SHOULD BE, KNOCK THAT PORK BACK INTO THE PAN WITH THE RESTING JUICES FROM WHATEVER YOU HAD IT RESTING IN, AND BRING BACK TO A SIMMER, YA WINNER.

NOW LET'S CHILL THE HEAT RIGHT THE FUCK DOWN AND BANG A LID ON IT, AND COOK FOR 2.5-3 HOURS, OR UNTIL YOU CAN PULL A PIECE OF PORK APART EASILY WITH A COUPLE OF FORKS.

DON'T FORGET TO CHECK ON YA STUFF EVERY NOW AND THEN, GIVE IT A STIR OCCASIONALLY AND MAKE SURE IT'S NOT STICKING TO THE BOTTOM OF THE PAN.

WHILE ALL THAT IS CARRYING ON, IT'S A RIPPER TIME TO MAKE THE GUACAMOLE. THERE'S HEAPS OF STUPID SHIT PEOPLE PUT IN GUACAMOLE AND SURE, SOMETIMES IT TASTES OKAY...

BUT PERSONALLY I LIKE THE MORE TRADITIONAL STYLE.

WELL, FUCK. . . IT'S PRETTY SMOOTH SAILING FROM HERE, LEGENDS. CHECK ON THAT PORK AT THE 2.5-HOUR MARK AND IF IT'S EASY TO FUCKEN BUST APART THEN WE ARE ED CHEERIN'. GRAB THOSE TRENDY FORKS OF YOURS, BUNG ON SOME MUMFORD AND SONS, STAMP ONE FOOT LOUDLY AS YOU GET READY TO PULL SOME PORK LIKE IT'S 2012, BABY.

2.5 HRS

LOUD AF!

SHHH

REMOVE THE POT FROM THE HEAT AND GET IN THERE AND SHRED THAT PORK TO BITS. BE WOWED BY HOW EASY THIS FUCKEN SHIT IS AND EVEN POSSIBLY AT HOW OLD YOU'VE GOTTEN IN THE LAST TEN YEARS.

BIG NIGHT ON THE TEA!

STIR THROUGH YOUR BEANS, A TABLESPOON OF BROWN SUGAR AND A PINCH OF SALT IF YOU THINK IT NEEDS IT.

WILL WAIT

SUGAR

IF IT'S TOO THIN A SAUCE FOR YOU, FEEL FREE TO CRANK THE HEAT BACK ON THE STOVE FOR A SECOND AND COOK IT DOWN A TOUCH.

GRAB YA GUAC AND YA PICKLE, THE 200 CLEVERLY NAMED HOT SAUCES THAT ARE FILLING UP YOUR FUCKEN PANTRY, CORIANDER LEAVES, GET THE BLOODY SOUR CREAM OUT AND OF COURSE SHRED YOUR BODY WEIGHT IN FUCKEN CHEESE RIGHT INTO A BOWL AND STICK IT ALL ON THE KITCHEN TABLE READY TO RAGE.

IF YOU FEEL LIKE REALLY REGRESSING, MAYBE EVEN GET AN IRRITATING HARD-TO-MANAGE CURLED-UP-CORN-CHIP-STYLE TACO SHELL, WRAP IT IN A SOFT ONE CAUSE IT'S NOT 1995 AND YOU NEED STRUCTURE IN YOUR LIFE THESE DAYS, AND FILL IT WITH ALL THAT STUFF HOWEVER THE FUCKEN BLOODY HELL YOU WANT.

IT'S TACO NIGHT SO GET YOUR MATES OVER AND PUNISH THEM WITH YOUR PASSÉ MUSIC TASTE WHILE YOU ALL EAT SO MANY FUCKEN TACOS YOU FEEL LIKE YOU MIGHT NEED TO CALL FOR HELP.

PIZZA PARTY

A →

C-60

STEREO

Who the bloody hell doesn't love pizza? A crowd-pleaser
if there ever was one. Then there is the old frozen
pizza wrapped in plastic with all the shit on it that
has slid to one side and cooks into a disappointing
hot cardboard UFO that tastes about as good as the
box it came in. Making your own pizza dough is
pretty fucken easy and so fucken cool, and you can
extend the recipe to suit a shitload of legends at once.
Definitely a big feeling of joy when you manage the
whole event yourself.

SERVES:
2
COOKING TIME:
about an hour

HECTOMETER: 6/10

KEY:
Impress the Judges | Kiddo Friendly

INGREDIENTS

DOUGH

300 G TIPO 'OO' FLOUR OR STRONG PLAIN FLOUR, PLUS EXTRA FOR DUSTING
3/4 CUP (180 ML) WARM WATER
BIG PINCH OF SEA SALT FLAKES
1 TEASPOON CASTER SUGAR
7 G SACHET DRIED YEAST
2 TABLESPOONS EXTRA VIRGIN OLIVE OIL
50 G SEMOLINA FLOUR OR POLENTA, TO DUST BENCH

PIZZA SAUCE

2 TABLESPOONS EXTRA VIRGIN
   OLIVE OIL
2 CLOVES GARLIC
SMALL HANDFUL FRESH
   BASIL LEAVES
1 TABLESPOON TOMATO PASTE
400 G CAN GOOD-QUALITY
   PEELED TOMATOES
   (SAN MARZANO IF POSSIBLE)
1/2 TEASPOON BROWN SUGAR
PINCH O' SALT

TOPPING

150 G MOZZARELLA (THE HARD
   STUFF, OR EVEN GRATED)
2 BALLS BUFFALO MOZZARELLA,
   TORN
150 G PROSCIUTTO
FRESH BASIL LEAVES
HANDFUL OF BABY ROCKET
SHAVE OF PARMESAN CHEESE,
   IF YOU LIKE
CHILLI FLAKES, OPTIONAL

(BUT ADD WHATEVER YOU LIKE,
IT'S YOUR BLOODY PIZZA, MATE)

JIM'SSS
WHOLE PEELED
TOMATOES

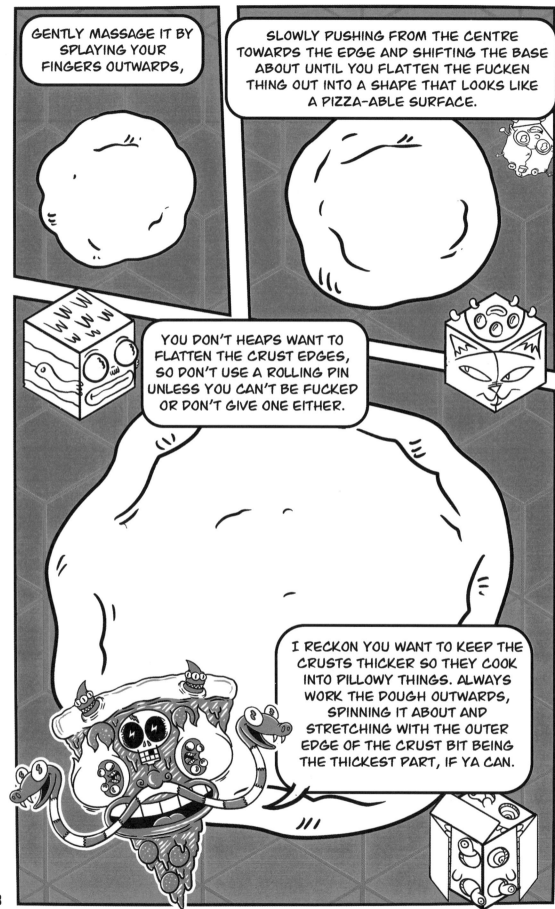

INDEX

PORK 'YEAH' BELLY

B SIDE

NOISE REDUCTION

IN
OUT

100 50 0

60

BIAS: NORMAL. EQUALISATION 120 μs

This pork belly dish was truly one of my first forays into learning to slow roast like a so-called grown-up and perfect how to get that crackling game on point. It was one of the first big bangers in my roasting repertoire and is still one of my favourites. I think I must have cooked it every other day for months, roping in as many people as I could to come to my place to serve it to them. The rad thing about the belly cut of meat is that it's fairly inexpensive and when you're trying to be a fancy pants on the dole, it ticks a big lot of boxes in that regard. It does unfortunately lend itself to ticking a few weight-gain boxes too when you fucken eat it four nights a week like I did at one stage. I developed the habit of getting a little obsessed with cooking the same thing to perfection for a hot second. It's certainly not an everyday dish this one, but also . . . do what ya fucken want, eh?

SERVES:
4–6
COOKING TIME:
just under 4 hours

HECTOMETER: 5/10

KEY:
Cheap AF | Impress the Judges | Low Stress

INGREDIENTS

- 1.5 KG PIECE BONELESS PORK BELLY
- 2 SMALL OR 1 LARGE ONION, PEELED AND SLICED INTO THICK RINGS
- 6–8 GARLIC CLOVES, PEELED AND BRUISED
- HANDFUL THYME LEAVES
- 1 TABLESPOON FENNEL SEEDS (ROUGHLY BUSTED APART IN A MORTAR AND PESTLE)
- OLIVE OIL
- SEA SALT FLAKES
- PEPPER
- 500 ML CHICKEN STOCK
- 250 ML BEER OR WHITE WINE
- 1 TABLESPOON PLAIN FLOUR

CRANK THE FUCK OUT OF THE OVEN TO 230°C FAN-FORCED (250°C CONVENTIONAL).

FUCKIN HOT!

230°

250°

GO DIG YOURSELF UP A NICE BONELESS PORK BELLY FROM YA LOCAL BUTCHER, AND PAT IT DRY SO THE SKIN IS NICE AND . . . WELL, DRY.

BUTCHER

PORK BELLY 1.5kg

NOW WE WANT TO SCORE THE PORK SKIN, AND BY THAT I DON'T MEAN GIVE IT A LITERAL NUMERICAL SCORE, NOR DO I EXPECT YOU TO ARRANGE A PIECE OF MUSIC FOR IT (THOUGH YOU ARE WELCOME TO DO SO). I MEAN WE WANNA CUT DOWN THE SKIN IN ROWS OR REALLY WHATEVER SHAPES OR DIRECTIONS YOU BLOODY LIKE. I FIND THAT NARROW ROWS HELP IT CRACKLE BETTER.

10

SICK RIFF!

YOU CAN OF COURSE GET YOUR BUTCHER TO DO THIS FOR YOU BUT IT'S HEAPS MORE FUN TO DO IT YOURSELF. YOU CAN'T EXPECT TO PROPERLY SCORE THE FUCKEN PORK SKIN WITH THE OLD DOGSHIT-SECOND-DRAWER-DOWN MAY-AS-WELL-BE-A-FUCKEN-SPOON BLUNT-AS-FUCK KNIFE. IT'S SHIT LIKE THAT THAT MAKES SO MANY PEOPLE LOSE THEIR COOL/LOVE FOR COOKING (GET A SHARPENER, THOUGH, AS A BLUNT KNIFE CAN BE WAY MORE DANGEROUS THAN A SHARP ONE, BELIEVE IT OR NOT).

YOU NEED SOME LETHALLY SHARP SHIT OTHERWISE YOU'RE GONNA RAGE QUIT THIS BIT.

FUCK JAR SAUCE

I LEARNED THIS TOUGH AF MOVE FROM JAMIE OLIVER AND IT'S A FUCKEN BEAUTY: GET A BOX CUTTER OR STANLEY KNIFE ETC., SET THE DEPTH TO SHALLOW AND NOT BRAVEHEART LENGTH. THE REASON YOU WANT IT SHALLOW IS YOU NEED TO CUT THROUGH THE PORK SKIN BUT NOT INTO THE PORK MEAT IF YOU CAN AVOID IT.

IT'S NO BIG DEAL IF YOU DO, BUT WAY BETTER IF YOU TRY TO JUST CUT THROUGH THE TOP LAYER OF SKIN AND INTO THE FAT LAYER. IN PARALLEL ROWS, SCORE THE WHOLE WAY FROM ONE END TO THE OTHER ALL OVER THE SKIN ANY DIRECTION YOU LIKE, IT SHOULD KIND OF RESEMBLE THE INTERCOOLER ON YOUR WRX ;).

IN AN OVENPROOF PAN A LITTLE BIGGER THAN THE BELLY, FANG IN YOUR ONIONS AND ON TOP SPRINKLE OVER THE GENTLY SQUASHED GARLIC AND THYME. YOU WANNA ARRANGE THE ONION IN A WAY THAT PROPS UP THE BELLY SO IT DOESN'T HAVE A SAG IN THE MIDDLE. IT WANTS TO BOW OUT LIKE A BELLY SHOULD.

OVENPROOF!

SO ADD MORE ONION TO ONE SIDE IF NEED BE. LAY THE BELLY ON THE ONIONS, GARLIC AND THYME. NEXT COME THE BASHED UP FENNEL SEEDS FOLLOWED BY A GOOD PINCH OF SALT FLAKES AND A CRACK OF PEPPER, WHICH YOU THEN RUB INTO THE SKIN AND SLITS YOU CUT WITH THE KNIFE. GIVE THE SKIN A LIGHT RUB WITH OLIVE OIL AND AN ADDITIONAL PINCH OF SALT IF YA LIKE.

CHICKEN

GLUG!

NEXT YOU TIP THE CHICKEN STOCK AND BOOZE INTO THE PAN AROUND THE PORK. IF IT LOOKS LIKE IT'S GONNA BE TOO FULL OR YOU'LL SWAMP THE SKIN, THEN STOP POURING, CHAMPION (NO OTHER STUPID SHIT ON THE SKIN NOW, PLEASE).

NOW TIME TO CRACKLE YOUR FAT.

THE CRACKLING MOSTLY HAPPENS IN THE FIRST SUPER-HOT BIT AND THEN CASUALLY MEANDERS ON A LOWER HEAT TO THE FINISH LINE. SO INTO THE OVEN FOR AROUND 40-45 MINUTES UNTIL THE SKIN IS BUBBLING UP AND IT'S STARTING TO LOOK LIKE FUCKEN CRACKLING.

FEEL FREE TO ROTATE THE TRAY IF YOU FEEL LIKE ONE SIDE OF THE FAT IS COPPING A FLOGGING TOO HARD.

AFTER THE 40ISH MARK, HEAT GOES THE ABSOLUTE FUCK DOWN TO 150°C FAN-FORCED (170°C CONVENTIONAL) FOR ANOTHER 2.5 HOURS. CHECK OCCASIONALLY AND TOP UP THE PAN WITH MORE STOCK IF IT LOOKS LIKE IT'S DRYING OUT.

MORE STOK?

ABSOLUTE FUCK DOWN

IF, AFTER ALL THAT CAREFUL TENDING OF THE CRACKLING, FOR SOME REASON YOU'RE NOT TOTALLY STOKED WITH YOUR LEVEL OF CRACKLE ON YA FAT, THEN YOU CAN BUNG IT UNDER THE GRILL FOR A SECOND BUT <u>DO NOT</u> WALK AWAY FROM IT, DON'T LEAVE ITS SIGHT OR YOU MAY FUCKEN OVERDO IT.

!!GRILL!!!

REMOVE THE BELLY FROM THE TRAY TO REST SOMEWHERE WARM, THEN STRAIN THE PAN JUICES INTO A SAUCEPAN AND SPOON OUT THE FATS/OILS THAT ARE FLOATING ON TOP (YOU CAN DISCARD THESE). BUNG IT OVER A MEDIUM HEAT AND SIMMER TO THICKEN.

OIL

FAT

MEDIUM

IN A SEPARATE BOWL MIX A BIT OF THAT COOKING LIQUID INTO THE FLOUR, WHISKING TO A PASTE THAT YOU THEN RETURN TO THE COOKING LIQUID. ADD MORE STOCK IF YOU WANT TO THIN IT OUT A BIT. AND THAT'S YA FUCKEN GRAVY, GREGORY.

FLOUR

YOU MAY FIND IT BENEFICIAL TO SLICE THE PORK ALONG THE ROWS YOU SCORED, AND/OR USE A SERRATED KNIFE.

GRAVY

SERVE WITH ROAST VEG (SEE GET FUCKED ROAST POTATOES) AND SOME GREEN VEGETABLES SO YOU DON'T SHIT YOURSELF FROM EATING SUPER RICH FOOD AND NOT ENOUGH FIBRE, CHAMPION.

THERE YOU GO, YA BLOODY FUCKEN LEGEND. ENJOY THAT MASSIVE WINNER OF A DINNER. YOU DESERVE IT.

RICE RICE BABY

I have made a shitload of soggy bowls of over-soy-sauced trash in my time, trying to get fried rice to land the way it should. It was a couple of small things that helped me make that dream come true. Firstly, last night's rice or cold, cooked rice was just the ticket that gave me the courage to fry another day. And secondly, a bit like a lot of great dishes, it doesn't need a huge number of additions to get it across the line. In fact, fewer ingredients makes it go way harder . . . ease up on the soy sauce, turbo.

SERVES:
4
COOKING TIME:
10–15 mins
(with pre-cooked rice)

HECTOMETER: 2.5/10

KEY:
Cheap AF | Kiddo Friendly | Low Stress | Quick Sticks

INGREDIENTS

4 CUPS COOKED WHITE RICE (COLD)
SHITLOAD OF GARLIC (6+ CLOVES), PEELED
I CARROT, PEELED
2 RED CHILLIES
4 FRENCH SHALLOTS (MORE EXPENSIVE, ANNOYING ONION), PEELED
250 G SPECK, BACON OR HAM (THE SAME WEIGHT OF GREEN BEANS, CAPSICUM AND CORN ARE RIPPER REPLACEMENTS FOR THE MEAT, IF YOU'RE VEGO)
2 EGGS
I CUP PEAS
VEG OR PEANUT OIL
2 TABLESPOONS OYSTER SAUCE (SUBSTITUTE MUSHROOM SAUCE OR EXCLUDE FOR VEG)
I-2 TABLESPOONS SOY SAUCE
3 SPRING ONIONS
SESAME OIL, TO SERVE (OPTIONAL)
CORIANDER AKA SOAP-TASTING POISON (OPTIONAL)

WHILE THE RICE IS COOLING,

CUT UP THE GARLIC,

CARROT,

CHILLI,

SHALLOTS

INTO MODERATELY SMALL SIZES THAT GIVE OFF A 'COOKS FAST' VIBE AND BUNG IT ALL IN A BOWL.

AND SPECK OR OTHER VEGGIES

CRACK YOUR EGGS INTO A BOWL

AND WH!SK TOGETHER.

NOW, OVER TO THE STOVE AND GET YOURSELF A SMALL PAN.

CHUCK IT ON MEDIUM-LOW AND BUNG IN SOME OIL

(WHEN I USED SESAME OIL HERE,

UNCLE ROGER TOLD ME OFF ON YOUTUBE AS IT SHOULDN'T REALLY BE HEATED UP,

SO USE VEG OR PEANUT OIL, IF YOU'D PREFER).

SELF PIE-SOLATION
SHEPHERD'S PIE
A →
C-60

Pie fixes everything, and this one was awesome
when stuck at home during lockdown. Who doesn't love
a bloody pie? Lamb mince is a total winner for this dish.
If you can't find lamb mince or the idea freaks you out for
some reason, use beef mince and call it a cottage pie.
One of the best fucking meals you'll ever eat right here.

SERVES:
6–8
COOKING TIME:
a couple of hours

HECTOMETER: 6/10

KEY:
Comfort Food | Feed the Team | Kiddo Friendly

FIRST CAB OFF THE RANK, YA WANNA FRY THE LAMB MINCE, BREAKING IT UP AS YOU GO. YOU WANT TO TRY AND COOK ALL THE LIQUID SHIT OUT OF IT. YOU'LL SEE LIQUID FORM AROUND THE MINCE- COOK IT OFF, WHEN THERE'S NO LIQUID LEFT AND THE MINCE HAS BROWNED, SCOOP IT OUT INTO A BOWL.

CHUCK YOUR PAN BACK ON THE HEAT, GIVE IT ANOTHER TABLESPOON OF OIL THEN BUNG IN THE ONION AND CARROT AND FRY IT FOR A FEW MINUTES TILL THEY'VE SOFTENED, THEN INTRODUCE THE LAMB BACK IN. GIVE THAT A STIR AND THEN CHUCK IN YOUR GARLIC. GIVE IT ANOTHER STIR AROUND. NEXT PUT IN YOUR TABLESPOON OF FLOUR. NOW, YA DO WANNA FRY IT OFF FOR A MINUTE OR TWO AFTER THIS, STIRRING CONTINUOUSLY, OTHERWISE YOU'LL TASTE THE FUCKEN FLOUR, AND FLOUR TASTES CHAT.

FUCK, THIS IS GOING TO TASTE GOOD AF.

IN GOES THE THYME. PULL THE ROSEMARY LEAVES OFF THE STALK AND CHUCK THOSE IN TOO. NEXT GIVE IT A GOOD GLUG OF WORCESTERSHIRE SAUCE AND BUNG IN A CUP OF STOUT. IF YA DON'T WANT TO USE STOUT, YOU CAN USE RED WINE, IT DOESN'T MATTER. COOK THE BOOZE OFF FOR A FEW MINUTES (5 ISH).

BUNG IN YA PEAS, GIVE IT A STIR. NEXT PUT IN A CUPPLA TABLESPOONS OF TOMATO PASTE. CHUCK IN A CUP OF BEEF STOCK... OR VEGGIE STOCK, OR CHICKEN STOCK OR WOODSTOCK. WHATEVER.

NOW,
IF YOU LIKE IT A BIT RICHER,
YOU CAN PUT MORE STOCK IN
AND SIMMER GENTLY
TO REDUCE THE AMOUNT OF LIQUID
IF YOU'VE GOT THE TIME.
ADD A LITTLE PINCH OF SALT
AND A CRACK OF PEPPER.
YOU WANNA SIMMER THIS
FOR A WHILE UNTIL IT'S THICK.
YOU DON'T WANNA
SEE HEAPS OF
RUNNY SHIT IN IT.
IT DOESN'T HAVE TO BE
STIFF AS A FUCKEN
BIRTHDAY CAKE,
BUT IT JUST NEEDS
TO BE STRUCTURALLY
SOUND ENOUGH TO BE
CONSIDERED A PIE.

CHECK ON YOUR POTATOES. IF THEY'RE SOFT ENOUGH TO STICK A FORK THROUGH EASILY, TAKE THEM OFF THE HEAT, DRAIN AND RETURN THEM TO THE WARM SAUCEPAN ON THE BENCH. ADD YA BUTTER, A BIG DASH OF CREAM OR MILK AND A PINCH OF SALT.

TO GET YOUR TWO EGG YOLKS YA GOTTA SEPARATE THE YOLKS FROM THE WHITES. EASIEST WAY TO DO THIS IS CRACK THE EGGS IN HALF AND HANG ONTO THE YOLK WITH HALF OF THE SHELL, THEN YA KINDA TIP IT BACK AND FORTH OVER A BOWL UNTIL YOU'RE LEFT WITH JUST THE YOLK AND THE WHITE HAS DRIPPED INTO THE BOWL. CHUCK THE YOLK IN WITH THE POTATOES AND DO THE SAME WITH THE OTHER EGG.

BANG IN YA CHEDDAR CHEESE, THEN MASH IT ALL TOGETHER. I LIKE TO USE A WHISK TO GET IT REALLY FUCKEN SMOOTH. RIGHTO, ONCE THAT'S DONE, CHECK ON YA MINCE. IF IT LOOKS LIKE IT'S KINDA HOLDING ITS SHAPE A BIT AND WITHOUT TOO MUCH LIQUID, THEN IT'S DONE.

WITH SOME SLOW, SEDUCTIVE MUSIC PLAYING, LOVINGLY TIP THE MINCE INTO THE PIE TRAY, EVEN IT OUT WITH A FUCKEN FLAT THING. OR A SPOON, WHATEVER TREVOR.

YEAH WHATEVER!

NEXT YOU WANNA TOP THE MINCE WITH MASHED POTATO, AND DON'T JUST FUCKEN PLONK IT ALL ON BECAUSE YOU'LL FUCK IT UP TRYING TO SQUISH IT DOWN. JUST DO A LITTLE AT A TIME. ONCE YOU'VE FINISHED YOUR LITTLE POTATO PLONK-A-RAMA, YOU WANT TO GENTLY SPREAD THE POTATO EVENLY ACROSS THE MINCE.

THEN GET YOURSELF A FORK AND DRAG IT ACROSS THE TOP OF THE PIE TO CREATE RIPPLES, DON'T ASK ME WHY, IT'S JUST THE WAY IT'S DONE. NEXT, GRATE A LITTLE PARMESAN CHEESE ON TOP, AND CHUCK IT IN THE OVEN FOR 25 MINUTES OR UNTIL IT'S A LITTLE GOLDEN BROWN ON TOP.

Just imagine a dish as therapeutic to eat as a lasagne, but instead of beef it's made with lamb and has layers of potato and eggplant as the pasta sheets . . . Imagine no more, champions! Moussaka is such a fucken rock 'n' roll dish, there are some incredible variations of it across the globe. Mine is based on the more traditional Greek style, as the combination of bechamel sauce and lamb mince suits me down to the bloody ground. The lamb and spice mix power combo will blow your bloody mind, and it'll no doubt be making a frequent appearance in your repertoire in no time. Get down and get with it, champions – it's worth every bit of effort, I swear.

SERVES:
6–8
COOKING TIME:
a few hours

HECTOMETER: 7/10

KEY:
Comfort Food | Feed the Team | Impress the Judges |
Worth the Effort

INGREDIENTS

2-3 EGGPLANTS (DEPENDING ON SIZE)

2 TABLESPOONS EXTRA VIRGIN OLIVE OIL, PLUS EXTRA TO DRIZZLE

3 TEASPOONS DRIED OREGANO

SEA SALT FLAKES

700G RED/DESIREE/DUTCH CREAM POTATOES (BUT ANY KIND ARE GOOD), SLICED INTO 1CM THICK SLICES

2 LARGE ONIONS, PEELED AND SLICED

2 BAY LEAVES

ALL THE GARLIC ON EARTH (A WHOLE BULB) SMASHED AND CHOPPED ROUGHLY AS YOU LIKE

1/3 TEASPOON GROUND ALL SPICE

1 TEASPOON GROUND CINNAMON

1 KG LAMB MINCE

SPRIG OF ROSEMARY

1 CUP RED WINE

½ CUP TOMATO PASTE

400G TIN PEELED WHOLE TOMATOES

2 TEASPOONS BROWN SUGAR

500 ML BEEF STOCK

PEPPER

½ CUP PANKO BREADCRUMBS OR REGULAR BREAD CRUMBS

LEMON WEDGES, TO SERVE

CHEESE BECHAMEL TOPPING

100G UNSALTED BUTTER

100G PLAIN FLOUR

750ML MILK

100G KEFALOGRAVIERA CHEESE, GRATED (OR PARMESAN)

FRESHLY GRATED NUTMEG OR ½ TEASPOON GROUND SHIT

SEA SALT FLAKES

FRESHLY GROUND PEPPER

2 EGGS, LIGHTLY BEATEN

GEAR

2 BAKING TRAYS

3.5 LITRE BAKING DISH

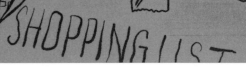

CHUCK A SICK 180°C FAN-FORCED (200°C CONVENTIONAL) AND GET THAT SHIT HEATING UP STRAIGHT OUT OF THE GATES.

THOSE BAKING TRAYS OF YOURS ARE GONNA NEED A WHACK OF BAKING PAPER OVER EACH OF THEM.

GRAB YOUR EGGPLANTS, CUT THE SILLY GREEN HATS OFF THEM AND SLICE INTO 1.5cm THIN ROUNDS.

LAY THEM ON THE BAKING TRAYS.

DRIZZLE OVER A LITTLE OIL FOLLOWED BY ONE TEASPOON DRIED OREGANO AND A PINCH OF SALT, THEN INTO THE OVEN AND WE ARE AWAY TO THE RACES.

IN 15-20 MINUTES, FLIP 'EM OVER, TREAT THEM TO ANOTHER PINCH OF SALT AND BELT 'EM BACK IN FOR THE SAME AMOUNT OF TIME UNTIL TENDER.

REMOVE THOSE TENDER MOMENTS FROM THE OVEN AND SET ASIDE.

PLACE YOUR POTATO SLICES INTO A SAUCEPAN OF <u>COLD</u> WATER PLEASE & THANK YOU AND BRING TO A SIMMER, COOKING UNTIL THE POTATO SLICES ARE TENDER —

8-10 MINUTES DEPENDING HOW THICK YOU WENT/TYPE OF POTATO ETC.

TRY NOT TO BOIL THE POTATOES UNTIL THE ABSOLUTE BULLSHIT HAS BEEN COOKED OUT OF THEM AND THEY'RE A PAIN IN THE ARSE TO WORK WITH.

GENTLY DRAIN AND SET ASIDE.

CRANK 2 TABLESPOONS OF YA OIL INTO A LARGE PAN, SAM, OVER A MEDIUM HEAT, AND THEN CHASE THAT WITH YOUR ONIONS AND BAY LEAVES FOR 3-4 MINUTES.

THEN IN GOES YOUR SHITLOAD OF GARLIC TO COOK FOR ANOTHER MINUTE,
FOLLOWED BY YOUR SPICES AND THE REMAINING OREGANO AND STIR TOGETHER.

GARLICKY SIDE NOTE:

I HAVE LEARNED A LOT ABOUT GARLIC OVER THE YEARS. THE BIGGEST BREAKTHROUGH HAS BEEN THE REALISATION THAT CUTTING IT UP SUPER FINE IS FOR THE MOST PART A WASTE OF FUCKING TIME UNLESS THE RECIPE CALLS FOR SAND-LIKE DICING OF THE GARLIC.
BE A LITTLE CASUAL ABOUT IT AND SEE HOW IT GOES FOR YA NEXT TIME. THE SHIT COOKS PRETTY QUICK; THE KINDA THICKER THE SLICES OF IT, THE LESS LIKELY THEY ARE TO BURN AND END UP TASTING ALL BITTER, PLUS BIG BITS OF BEAUTIFUL COOKED GARLIC IN YOUR MEAL IS OFTEN FUCKEN
— RIGHTEOUS.

CRANK THE HEAT UP A TOUCH,

BUNG IN YOUR MINCE AND FRY FOR AROUND 10 MINUTES OR UNTIL IT HAS A NICE BIT OF COLOURING TO IT AND ANY WATERY NONSENSE HAS LEFT THE BUILDING. AS YOU NEAR THE END OF THIS STAGE, I LIKE TO CHUCK IN A HANDFUL OF ROSEMARY LEAVES OR EVEN THE WHOLE SPRIG.

IN GOES THE CUP OF REDDERS, COOK THE BOOZE OFF FOR 2-3 MINUTES, THEN FOLLOW THAT WITH YOUR TOMATO PASTE, TINNED WHOLE TOMATOES, BROWN SUGAR AND STOCK. STIR, BRING TO A SIMMER, REDUCE THE HEAT, FANG A LID ON AND COOK FOR 30 MINUTES.

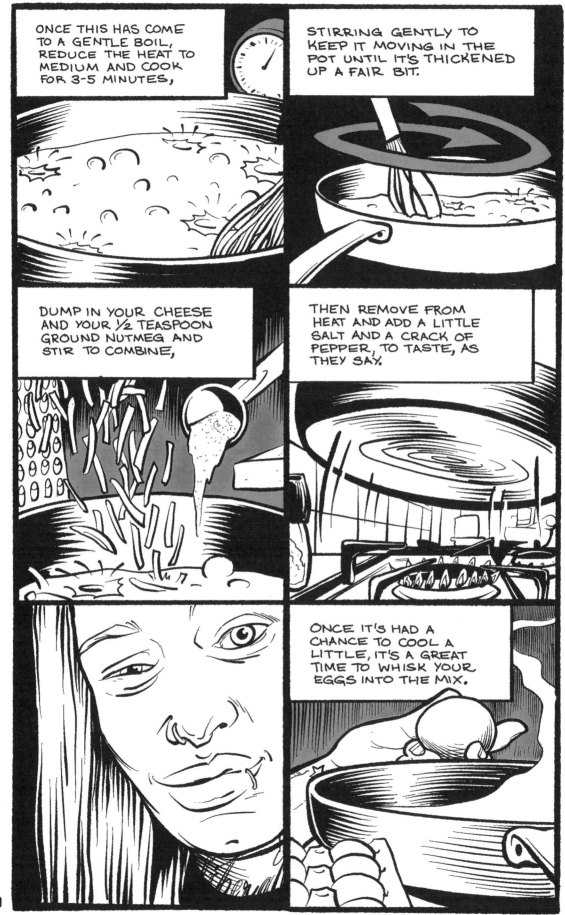

IF YOU FORGOT TO TURN YOUR OVEN OFF EARLIER THAT'S OKAY 'CAUSE WE'RE GONNA TURN IT THE FUCK BACK ON TO 180°C FAN-FORCED (200°C CONVENTIONAL.)

ABOUT A 3.5 LITRE CAPACITY BAKING DISH WILL BE STERLING FOR THIS NEXT STAGE. GRAB IT AND LET'S MAKE THIS BLOODY LEGENDARY THING HAPPEN.

EASY AS YA LIKE PLACE AROUND A THIRD OF THE LAMB MIXTURE INTO THE DISH, REMOVING ANY BAY LEAVES OR ROSEMARY STEMS IF YOU SPOT THEM.

THEN LAY ON ALL YOUR EVER-SO-TENDER POTATOES TO FORM A LAYER, AND ON TOP OF THAT GOES ANOTHER THIRD OF THE LAMB MIXTURE.

DON'T WORRY IF YOU CAN SEE A LITTLE POTATO PEEKING THROUGH THE MEAT SAUCE. IT MAY SEEM LIKE THERE ISN'T ENOUGH SAUCE, BUT TRUST ME, IT COOKS TOGETHER LIKE A FUCKEN DREAM.

NOW ON TOP OF THAT, HIT IT WITH THE EGGPLANT; AND THEN AGAIN WITH THE REMAINING LAMB SAUCE.

NOW WITH SOME KIND OF APPROPRIATELY CHEESY TUNES PLAYING, GENTLY TIP OVER YOUR BECHAMEL AND TRY AS HARD AS YOU CAN NOT TO SUDDENLY TIP IT INTO YOUR MOUTH BECAUSE IT LOOKS SO FUCKING GOOD RN OMG.

So, just so you got it right, from the bottom of the dish upwards the layers should go a little something like this:

SAUCE
POTATO
SAUCE
EGGPLANT
SAUCE
BECHAMEL

Even the bechamel out across the top and scatter with your breadcrumbs, a little salt and a crack of pepper.

Bung in the oven for 35-45 mins until golden on top and bubbling about like a bloody tasty champion.

With that said, the dish may bubble some tasty rad shit over the side, so having a tray under it might not be a shit idea unless you are the only person on earth who actually enjoys cleaning ovens.

I reckon lamb shanks are an unstoppably rock'n'roll
feed. I mean, what's more rock'n'roll than having
a bone on yer plate with meat hanging off it, that's been
cooked in booze and served on a bed of pulverised potato?
I don't know anyone who doesn't like them, either
(unless that person's a vego, of course). They're always
a bloody crowd pleaser. Even if you overcook the
shit out of them they still taste amazing. There're
a few cheeky tricks I like to use but this is really
just a classic hits dish.

SERVES:
4
COOKING TIME:
2.5–3-ish hours

HECTOMETER: 4.5/10

KEY:
Comfort Food │ Feed the Team │ Impress the Judges

INGREDIENTS

1 CARROT, PEELED
1 ONION, PEELED
2 STICKS CELERY
1 ENTIRE BULB GARLIC, PEELED (I LOVE FUCKEN GARLIC, BUT
IF YOU'RE LESS OF A FAN, USING 4-6 CLOVES WILL STILL
WORK)
4 LAMB SHANKS
SALT AND PEPPER
1 CUP FLOUR
CUPPLA TABLESPOONS OLIVE OIL
1 CUP RED WINE
2 TABLESPOONS TOMATO PASTE
CUPPLA STICKS OF LOCAL (FLOGGED) ROSEMARY
3-4 CUPS BEEF STOCK
1 TABLESPOON BALSAMIC VINEGAR
2 TABLESPOONS WORCESTERSHIRE SAUCE
1 TABLESPOON BROWN SUGAR
1.5 KG POTATOES
2 TABLESPOONS BUTTER
1 CUP MILK

MOO!

TOMATO PASTE!

I LOVE GETTIN' MASHED!

WOR CESTER SHIRE SAUCE

BAL SAMIC VINEGAR

NEVER PAY!

GOON

IF YOU CAN BE FUCKED, DUST THE LAMB SHANKS IN THE SALT, PEPPER AND FLOUR AND BROWN OFF IN THE PAN FOR A SEC IN A LITTLE OLIVE OIL, THEN REMOVE AND SET ASIDE, (DON'T STRESS TOO MUCH ABOUT THIS, BUT IT ADDS A RICHNESS TO THE FLAVOUR AND CAN HELP KICK THINGS UP A NOTCH.)

IN THE SAME PAN SAUTÉ THE CONTENTS OF THE BOWL IN A LITTLE MELTED BUTTER FOR FIVE MINUTES OR UNTIL IT STARTS TO BROWN.

RETURN THE SHANKS TO THE POT.

ADD A BIG GLUG OF RED WINE AND COOK THE BOOZE OFF FOR A COUPLE OF MINUTES.

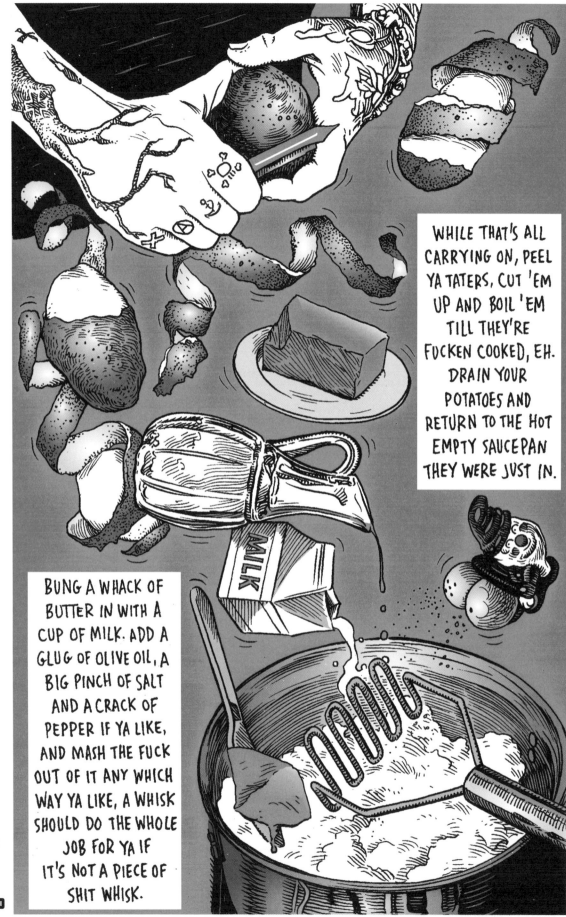

WHILE THAT'S ALL CARRYING ON, PEEL YA TATERS, CUT 'EM UP AND BOIL 'EM TILL THEY'RE FUCKEN COOKED, EH. DRAIN YOUR POTATOES AND RETURN TO THE HOT EMPTY SAUCEPAN THEY WERE JUST IN.

BUNG A WHACK OF BUTTER IN WITH A CUP OF MILK. ADD A GLUG OF OLIVE OIL, A BIG PINCH OF SALT AND A CRACK OF PEPPER IF YA LIKE, AND MASH THE FUCK OUT OF IT ANY WHICH WAY YA LIKE, A WHISK SHOULD DO THE WHOLE JOB FOR YA IF IT'S NOT A PIECE OF SHIT WHISK.

AFTER THE 2 HOURS ARE UP, GINGERLY REMOVE THE SHANKS. TRY TO KEEP THE MEAT ON THE BONES, COVER AND LEAVE TO REST. CRANK THE HEAT BACK UP A BIT AND REDUCE THE REMAINING SAUCE FOR ABOUT 15 MINUTES, STIRRING OCCASIONALLY.

TURN THE HEAT OFF THE SAUCE. SPOON THE MASH ONTO FOUR PLATES. PLACE THE FUCKEN SHANK WITH THE FANCY BONE STILL IN IT ON THE MASH, DUH. THEN LADLE OVER THE SAUCE.

RECOMMENDED: DRINK RED WINE AND TALK SHIT WITH DINNER.

AND THERE YOU HAVE IT... A GET-FUCKED RIPPER OF A FEED.

SACRIFICIAL LAMB RACK

A
C-60

STEREO

This recipe is so crazy tasty you'll think you died and went to hell/heaven. I wanted to create a dish that gave off a real death metal energy while tasting like something you'd eat at a flash restaurant. Jules and I filmed an episode featuring this recipe in the middle of Sydney's lockdown. We went all-out and green-screened the whole kitchen to make it look like it was set in a fiery pit of doom. It was one of the biggest efforts I'd ever made for a video, and it took me the better part of two weeks to edit the fucken thing, too. Entirely worth it, and unlike the video production, the dish is as easy as all get out.

SERVES:
2
COOKING TIME:
30 mins prep, 30 mins cooking

HECTOMETER: 6/10

KEY:
Impress the Judges

INGREDIENTS

- 1–1.2 KG LAMB RACK
- 4 LONG RED CHILLIES
- 2 TABLESPOONS OLIVE OIL
- PARSLEY, TO SERVE

SWEET POTATO MASH
- 2 MEDIUM SWEET POTATOES (800G APPROX.)
- 1 WHOLE BULB GARLIC
- 20 G BUTTER
- SALT AND PEPPER
- SPLASH OF CREAM OR FULL-CREAM MILK

JUS
- 3–4 FRENCH SHALLOTS OR 1 RED ONION
- 4–6 GARLIC CLOVES, PEELED AND DICED
- 30 G BUTTER
- 150 ML RED WINE
- 150 ML BEEF STOCK
- 1 TABLESPOON BROWN SUGAR

STRAIGHT OUT OF HELL'S GATE, YOU'RE GONNA NEED TO SUMMON THE HEAT IN THE OVEN TO A BRUTAL 200°C FAN-FORCED (220°C CONVENTIONAL).

PROCEED TO WASH ANY DIRT AND BULLSHIT OFF YOUR SWEET POTATOES, THEN DRY THEM. PRICK A BUNCH OF HOLES IN THEM WITH A FORK, BUT DON'T FUCKEN STAB YOURSELF, PLEASE! WRAP IN FOIL AND THEN DROP KICK THEM INTO THE OVEN FOR 45–60 MINUTES. YOU'LL KNOW WHEN THEY'RE DONE 'CAUSE YOU SHOULD BE ABLE TO EASILY STICK A PITCHFORK OR SMALL TRIDENT THROUGH THEM.

IF YOU WANNA TURN THIS SHIT UP TO 11 ON THE FANCY-PANTOMETER, YOU CAN EMPLOY THE BRUTAL TECHNIQUE OF 'FRENCHING' THE BONES, AKA CLEANING/SCRAPING THE BONES WITH A KNIFE TO REMOVE ALL FAT AND EXCESS MEAT AND ONLY LEAVING THE EYE OF THE CUTLET ON THE NOW-EXPOSED BONE.

Frenching

FANCY-PANTOMETER

I'LL BE HONEST, THIS PROCESS IS A BIT OF FUCKING AROUND AND NOT ENTIRELY NECESSARY BUT IT DOES LOOK KINDA COOL.

TO PREP THE JUS INGREDIENTS, PEEL AND CHOP/SLICE YOUR SHALLOTS/RED ONION ALONG WITH YOUR GARLIC CLOVES, AND CHUCK IN A BOWL OF THEIR OWN.

INTERNAL LAMB TEMPERATURE CHART TO HELP YOU KNOW WHERE YOU'RE AT.

MED WELL DONE
MEDIUM
MED RARE
RARE

55°C RARE
55–60°C MEDIUM RARE
60–65°C MEDIUM
65°C MEDIUM WELL DONE

65°C+ ONWARDS IS PRETTY MUCH GONNA MAKE IT WHAT I IMAGINE TO BE SIMILAR TO TRYING TO CHEW THE INNER TUBE OUT OF A BMX, BUT I GET IF SEEING PINK IN THE MEAT FREAKS YOU OUT, SO BY ALL MEANS COOK PAST THAT TEMP AT YOUR HELLISH LEISURE.

REDLINE

USING THE SAME PAN YOU JUST SEARED YOUR LAMB IN, TURN THE HEAT DOWN TO MEDIUM-HIGH AND MELT 30 G BUTTER, THEN DROP IN THE PRE-CHOPPED SHALLOTS/ONION AND GARLIC AND SAUTÉ OR SWEAT THEM FOR A FEW MINUTES UNTIL THEY SOFTEN AND BEGIN TO TURN BROWN. WHILE THE LAMB IS IN THE OVEN, LET'S MAKE THE JUS.

ADD THE RED POTION (WINE) TO THE PAN, BEING CAREFUL IT DOESN'T CATCH THE LIP OF THE PAN AND CATCH FIRE (UNLIKE ME, WHO INTENTIONALLY DID IT ON CAMERA TO LOOK COOL), AND COOK FOR 2-3 MINUTES.

POUR IN YOUR BEEF STOCK ALONG WITH THE BROWN SUGAR AND SIMMER GENTLY FOR 7-10 MINUTES UNTIL THE LIQUID HAS REDUCED BY ABOUT HALF. THEN STRAIN THE WHOLE LOT THROUGH A SIEVE INTO A BOWL TO SEPARATE THE LIQUID FROM THE ONION AND GARLIC.

MAKE SURE TO GIVE THESE LUMPY BITS A GOOD FUCKEN PUSH THROUGH THE SIEVE TO GET ALL THE GOOD FLAVOURS OUT OF THEM INTO THAT BOWL. THEN, WOULD YOU BELIEVE IT, WE CHUCK THE LIQUID PART BACK IN THE PAN AND COOK IT DOWN EVEN MORE UNTIL IT'S THICKENED ENOUGH TO COAT THE BACK OF A SPOON. THE CONSISTENCY SHOULD BE KINDA THINNER THAN HONEY BUT THICKER THAN WINE, IF THAT MAKES SENSE?

30g BUTTER

BEEF STOCK

SUGAR

SIMMER

7-11 MINS

LUCI'S RED POTION

IF WE HAVE TIMED IT RIGHT, OUT OF THE OVEN SHOULD COME EVERYTHING (UNLESS SOMETHING LOOKS OR FEELS LIKE IT NEEDS LONGER, IN WHICH CASE LEAVE IT IN FOR A SEC).

EVERYTHING

REST THE LAMB IN A WARM PLACE. YOU CAN COVER IT WITH FOIL IF YOU LIKE OR DON'T HAVE ANYWHERE YOU CONSIDER THAT WARM.

CAREFULLY PEEL THE SKINS OFF THE CHILLIES TO KEEP THEM WHOLE. SET ASIDE.'

UNWRAP THE FOIL FROM THE SWEET POTATOES AND SCRAPE OUT THE ORANGE SHIT FROM INSIDE THE SKINS INTO A BOWL. REMOVE THE FOIL FROM THE GARLIC BULB AND SQUEEZE THE COOKED GARLIC CLOVES INTO THE SWEET POTATO FLESH WITH 20G BUTTER, A DASH OF CREAM OR MILK AND A CRACK OF SALT AND PEPPER.

WHISK TOGETHER WITH A MASHER OR EVEN BETTER . . . YEP, A WHISK!

GIVE THAT MASH POTATO LOVE UNTIL THERE ARE FEW TO NO LUMPS. ADD MORE SALT AND PEPPER IF YA WANT, AND IF IT'S TOO THICK ADD MORE MILK (BUT SLOWLY, OR IT WILL TURN TO SOUP).

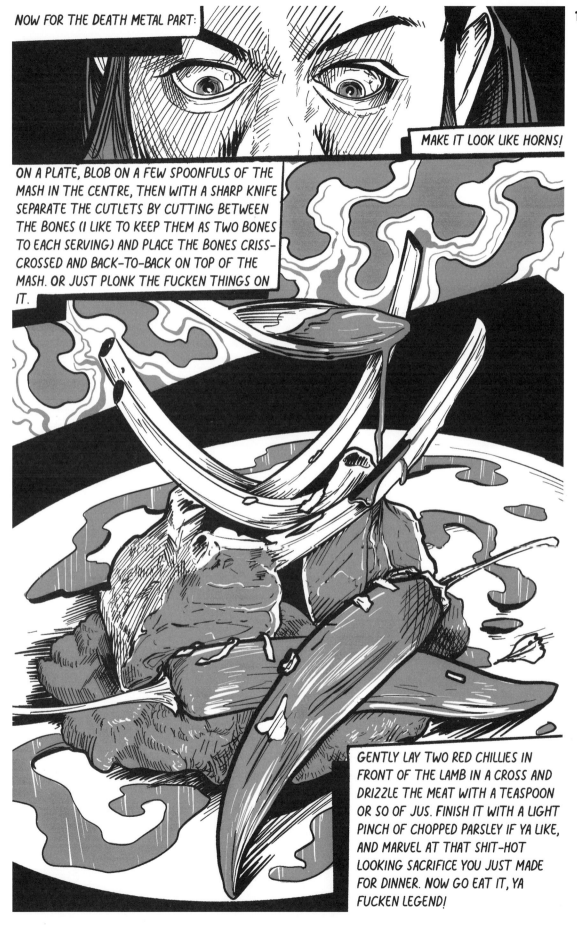

NOW FOR THE DEATH METAL PART:

MAKE IT LOOK LIKE HORNS!

ON A PLATE, BLOB ON A FEW SPOONFULS OF THE MASH IN THE CENTRE, THEN WITH A SHARP KNIFE SEPARATE THE CUTLETS BY CUTTING BETWEEN THE BONES (I LIKE TO KEEP THEM AS TWO BONES TO EACH SERVING) AND PLACE THE BONES CRISS-CROSSED AND BACK-TO-BACK ON TOP OF THE MASH. OR JUST PLONK THE FUCKEN THINGS ON IT.

GENTLY LAY TWO RED CHILLIES IN FRONT OF THE LAMB IN A CROSS AND DRIZZLE THE MEAT WITH A TEASPOON OR SO OF JUS. FINISH IT WITH A LIGHT PINCH OF CHOPPED PARSLEY IF YA LIKE, AND MARVEL AT THAT SHIT-HOT LOOKING SACRIFICE YOU JUST MADE FOR DINNER. NOW GO EAT IT, YA FUCKEN LEGEND!

This was my response to seeing those fucken vomitus yellow jars of pre-made curry sauce that look closer to baby shit than they do dinner. Now, when I say Mild Curry, the 'mild' part of that statement is really up to you and how spicy you and the gang are feeling today: it can be taken from mild to wild-child real fast – it's all in the amount of chilli and NOT in the rest of the spices! Rightyo, time to channel your inner ex-Australian Prime Minister energy and make everyone curry (but cook the chicken the whole way through this time).

SERVES:
4–6
COOKING TIME:
about an hour

HECTOMETER: 5/10

KEY:
Cheap AF | Feed the Team | Quick Sticks

INGREDIENTS

1 TEASPOON TURMERIC
1 TEASPOON GARAM MASALA
1/4 TEASPOON GROUND CINNAMON
PINCH OF SALT
600ISH G BONELESS SKINLESS CHICKEN THIGHS
2 RED CAPSICUMS
1 RED ONION, PEELED
1 LARGE RED OR GREEN CHILLI (DESEEDED IF YOU HAVE A DEEP FEAR OF CHILLI, OR LEAVE OUT ALTOGETHER)
WHOLE HEAD OF GARLIC, PEELED
BIG THUMB OF GINGER
VEGETABLE OIL
5 CARDAMOM PODS
2 TINS CRUSHED TOMATOES
1 CUP OF CHICKEN STOCK
BAY LEAVES
1/2 CUP THICKENED CREAM/COCONUT CREAM/COCONUT MILK
1-2 TEASPOONS BROWN SUGAR (OPTIONAL)
EXTRA SPICE DURING COOKING:
HEAPED TEASPOON GARAM MASALA
1/2-1 TEASPOON CHILLI POWDER

YOGO BLOB

1 CUP GREEK OR NATURAL YOGHURT
1/2 TEASPOON GROUND CORIANDER
1/2 TEASPOON GROUND CUMIN
SQUEEZE OF LEMON JUICE
PINCH OF SALT
SMALL BUNCH FRESH CORIANDER, CHOPPED (OPTIONAL)
1 1/2 CUPS BASMATI PANTS RICE, TO SERVE

BUST YA CARDAMOM PODS OPEN WITH THE BACK OF A SPOON OR A PAN OR YA BLOODY HEAD TO LET THE SEEDS INSIDE GO FREE TO GET INVOLVED, OTHERWISE IT'S LIKE COOKING A BANANA WITH THE SKIN ON (THE GOOD SHIT IS INSIDE THE POD).

THROW THE PAN BACK ONTO THE MEDIUM-HIGH HEAT WITH A TABLESPOON MORE OF OIL AND FRY THE CARDAMOM SEEDS FOR 20 SECONDS OR SO, THEN CHASE THEM IN WITH THE PREPARED VEGGIES. COOK THAT FUCKEN SHIT FOR 3-5 MINUTES TILL THE ONIONS HAVE STARTED TO TURN TRANSLUCENT.

NOW ADD A HEAPED TEASPOON OF ADDITIONAL GARAM MASALA AND ½ TEASPOON OR AS-MUCH-AS-YOU-ARE-TOUGH-ENOUGH-FOR CHILLI POWDER.

FRY OFF THESE SPICES FOR ANOTHER 2 MINUTES AND THEN ADD THE GINGER AND COOK FOR A FURTHER 2 MINUTES.

ADD THE BROWNED CHICKEN, FOLLOWED BY YOUR TOMATOES AND A CUP OF STOCK. THROW IN A FEW BAY LEAVES FOR REASONS ONLY UNDERSTOOD BY THE BAY LEAF LOVERS SOCIETY...

I'VE SAID IT SEVERAL TIMES BEFORE: I'M CONVINCED THE ONLY REASON THEY GO IN FOOD IS TO MAKE YOU LOOK LIKE YOU KNOW WHAT YOU'RE DOING, UNLIKE SHARE-HOUSE SHANE AND HIS 4 KG SACK OF CURRY POWDER.

CURRY

WINNER, WINNER ROAST CHICKEN DINNER

I made thirteen of these for a mate's wedding once in 36-degree heat. I cooked them in a tiny portable woodfired pizza oven on the back of a trailer. The oven was way too fucken hot and could only fit three chickens in it at once but they all turned out perfect and everyone loved them. The only failure was when I carried out the last tray of carved chicken to the guests, tripped on a fucken guide rope for the reception tent and threw chicken all over the lawn. Devvo.

SERVES:
4–6
COOKING TIME:
depends on the size
of your chicken,
1.5–2 hours on average

HECTOMETER: 4.5/10

KEY:
Feed the Team | Kiddo Friendly

INGREDIENTS

1 FREE-RANGE CHICKEN (ANY SIZE YA LIKE)
2 RED ONIONS
GARLIC
BUTTER
2 ORANGES
THYME
OLIVE OIL
SALT AND PEPPER
SMOKED PAPRIKA
COOKING TWINE
CHICKEN STOCK
1½ TABLESPOONS PLAIN FLOUR

GET THE OVEN CRANKING TO 200ºC (180-190ºC IF IT'S FAN FORCED).

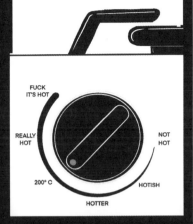

GRAB THAT CHICKEN AND PAT IT DRY WITH SOME PAPER TOWEL INSIDE AND OUT.

MAKE SURE THERE AREN'T ANY GUTS IN IT, AND IF THERE ARE THEN REMOVE THEM.

PEEL AND SLICE YOUR ONIONS INTO THICK RINGS AND LINE A BAKING DISH WITH THEM.

PEEL A COUPLE OF CLOVES OF GARLIC AND SLICE INTO THIN FLAT SLICES.

NEXT COMES A TRICK YOU MIGHT NOT HAVE DONE BEFORE, BUT IT'S EASY ONCE YOU'VE DONE IT A FEW TIMES: WE WANNA TRY TO LIFT THE SKIN OFF THE BREAST AND STUFF BUTTER AND GARLIC BETWEEN THE SKIN AND FLESH.

1 GET THE CHOOK BREAST-SIDE UP WITH THE DRUMSTICK END FACING YOU.

2 IN THE MIDDLE WILL BE THE HIGHEST PART OF THE BREAST.

3 YA WANNA GENTLY LIFT THE SKIN UPWARDS FROM THE FURTHEST TIP OF THE BREAST SO YOU SEE IT COME AWAY FROM THE FLESH SLIGHTLY.

4 USING YOUR FINGER OR THE UNDERSIDE OF A DESSERT SPOON (BEING CAREFUL NOT TO TEAR THE SKIN)...

5 TRY TO GET INTO THAT GAP TO FURTHER LOOSEN THE SKIN FROM THE MEAT – YOU MAY NEED TO BUST THROUGH A THIN LAYER OF ADJOINING SKIN TO MAKE IT, BUT YOU SHOULD BE ABLE TO CREATE A LITTLE POCKET ON BOTH THE LEFT AND RIGHT SIDES OF THE BREAST BONE, LEAVING THE MIDDLE SEAM INTACT.

6 THEN STUFF THAT WITH AS MUCH BUTTER AS YOU LIKE (A TABLESPOON-ISH EACH SIDE SHOULD GET YOU OUT OF TROUBLE), AND SQUEEZE THOSE FLAT SLICES OF GARLIC IN TOO (ABOUT A CLOVE OR TWO ON EACH SIDE).

ONE WAY

ENTER

7 RIPPER. NOW CUT ONE ORANGE IN HALF AND BUNG ONE HALF IN THE CAVITY OF THE CHICKEN WITH A BUNCH OF PEELED GARLIC. SLIDE IN A BUNCH OF THYME ON TOP OF IT ALL.

NOW WE WANNA COVER THE WHOLE BLOODY CHICKEN WITH OLIVE OIL, SALT, PEPPER AND PAPRIKA. GIVE IT A GOOD FUCKEN RUB TILL THE WHOLE BIRD IS KINDA RED WITH THE PAPRIKA.

(FUCK IT LOOKS GOOD ALREADY, HEY? DON'T EAT IT YET THOUGH.)

NOW PLACE THE CHICKY BIRD ON THE ONIONS AND CUT YOURSELF ENOUGH OF A LENGTH OF COOKING TWINE TO TIE THE LEGS TOGETHER. YOU DON'T NEED TO BIND THEM OVER EACH OTHER SO IT LOOKS LIKE IT'S BEING HELD HOSTAGE, TRUST ME – IT WON'T ESCAPE THE OVEN: JUST ENOUGH TO HOLD THEM AGAINST THE BREAST.

WITH THE REMAINING ORANGE, SQUEEZE THE JUICE INTO THE DISH AND THEN POUR ABOUT A CM OF CHICKEN STOCK INTO THE TRAY.

IF YOU'RE SERVING ROAST VEGGIES WITH THE CHICKEN, PAR BOIL THEM IN A SAUCEPAN OF WATER AND FANG THEM ON THEIR OWN TRAY AND TOSS THEM WITH SOME OLIVE OIL, SALT, PEPPER AND THYME.

YOU BEAUTY, BUNG IT ALL IN THE OVEN.

NOW EVERY 20 MINUTES YOU WANNA BASTE THE CHICKEN WITH THE PAN JUICE. DON'T SKIP THIS SHIT, IT'S A POWER MOVE.

DEPENDING ON ITS SIZE, THE CHICKEN WILL BE COOKED IN ABOUT 1¼ TO 1½ HOURS – RECKON ON ABOUT 25 MINS PER 500 G. YOU'LL KNOW THE CHICKEN IS DONE COS WHEN YOU POKE THE THIGHS WITH A KNIFE, CLEAR LIQUID WILL RUN FROM THEM. IF YOU WANNA PLAY IT SAFE AND HAVE A FANCY MEAT THERMOMETER, JAB IT INTO THE CHICKEN BREAST AND IF IT READS 75ºC OR MORE YOU'RE SAFE AS HOUSES.

ONCE THAT'S SORTED, REMOVE THE CHICKEN FROM THE OVEN AND LET IT REST.

IF YOUR VEGGIES AREN'T BROWN ENOUGH FOR YA, THEN CRANK THE HEAT UP A BIT WHILE THE BIRD RELAXES.

GRAVY TIME

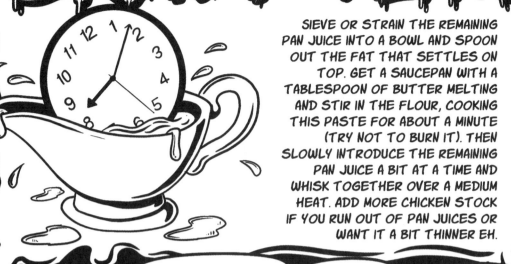

SIEVE OR STRAIN THE REMAINING PAN JUICE INTO A BOWL AND SPOON OUT THE FAT THAT SETTLES ON TOP. GET A SAUCEPAN WITH A TABLESPOON OF BUTTER MELTING AND STIR IN THE FLOUR, COOKING THIS PASTE FOR ABOUT A MINUTE (TRY NOT TO BURN IT). THEN SLOWLY INTRODUCE THE REMAINING PAN JUICE A BIT AT A TIME AND WHISK TOGETHER OVER A MEDIUM HEAT. ADD MORE CHICKEN STOCK IF YOU RUN OUT OF PAN JUICES OR WANT IT A BIT THINNER EH.

REMOVE VEGGIES FROM THE OVEN IF YA MADE THEM.

AFTER YOU CARVE YOUR BIRD, SQUEEZE THE ORANGE FROM THE CAVITY OF THE CHICKEN OVER THE MEAT.

THERE YA HAVE IT. PERFECT EVERY TIME CHICKEN ... SO EAT IT.

TELL ME IT'S NOT THE BEST YOU'VE EVER HAD, I BET YA WON'T.

CHICKEN PARMY

A →

C-60

STEREO

Whether you call it a Parmy or a Parma and have
it with or without ham, I think we can all agree that
it's a smash hit for a bloody good reason. Let us embrace
this powerful pub classic in all its calorific glory:
the mighty chicken parmigiana.

SERVES:
2–4
COOKING TIME:
about an hour
(or 1.5-ish hours if you need
to make the sauce as well)

HECTOMETER: 4/10

KEY:
Comfort Food | Kiddo Friendly

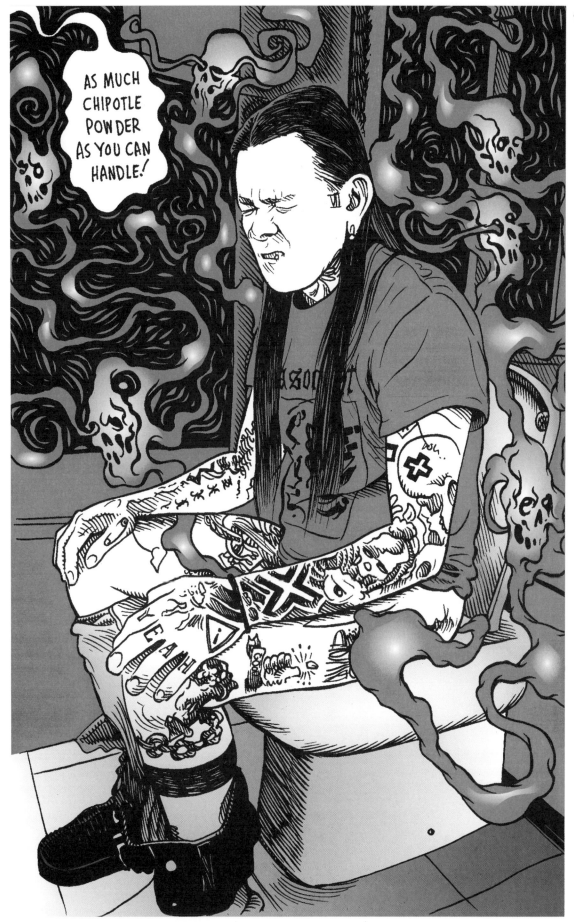

NOW FOR THE FUN BIT. WITH A BIG FLAT THING LIKE A FRYING PAN OR THE BACK END OF A GUITAR, GIVE THE BREASTS A SMACK UNTIL THEY'RE ALL FLATTENED OUT EVENLY SO ONE END ISN'T THICKER THAN THE OTHER IF THAT MAKES SENSE?

DON'T GO TOO BANANAS, HERCULES, YOU STILL WANT THEM IN ONE PIECE.

NEXT DUST EACH PIECE OF MEAT FIRST IN FLOUR, THEN DIP IN THE EGG WASH AND FINALLY THE BREADCRUMB MIXTURE. SET ASIDE AND FUCK OFF OVER TO THE STOVE, CHAMPION.

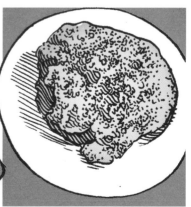

BOND EYE CHICKEN BURGER

(HOLD THE SAND)

Surf's up, Bond fans, 'cause this dish has nothing to do with surfing or being a secret pest. Rather, it's a dish known well in Sydney and around certain infamous iconic sandy bodies of water. If you have travelled to specific famous beaches and their respective fast-food joints anywhere from the late 90s through to today, you may have come across burgers called a 'Portuguese Style Chicken Burger'. When I first discovered them, these peri-peri sauce smothered chicken burgers with their mayo, chilli and cheese nonsense were so fucken mind-blowingly rad that I almost didn't know what to do with myself. This is my homage to one of the best fucken chicken burgers ever created. I hope you dig my Jamesless Bond Eye Burger, champions. It's a fucken winner, trust me.

SERVES:
4
COOKING TIME:
easily under an hour

HECTOMETER:
with mayo 7/10 | without 5/10

KEY:
Cheap AF | Worth the Effort

INGREDIENTS

500 G SKINLESS CHICKEN BREASTS.
OLIVE OIL

CHICKEN MARINADE

1 LEMON (ZEST AND JUICE)
4 - 6 GARLIC CLOVES, PEELED
30 ML OLIVE OIL
½ TSP SMOKED PAPRIKA
1 LONG RED CHILLI
2 BIRD'S EYE CHILLIES
BIG PINCH O' SALT
PINCH FRESH OREGANO LEAVES
1 TEASPOON BROWN SUGAR

CHILLI SAUCE

1 LEMON (ZEST AND JUICE)
1 BAY LEAF
4 GARLIC CLOVES, PEELED
30 ML OLIVE OIL
PINCH FRESH OREGANO LEAVES
½ TEASPOON SMOKED PAPRIKA
1 LONG RED CHILLI
6 - 8 BIRD'S EYE CHILLIES
BIG PINCH O' SALT
1 TEASPOON BROWN SUGAR
HALF A RED ONION, PEELED
AND ROUGHLY CHOPPED

MAYO

1 EGG YOLK (NOT THE WHITE)
300 ML GRAPESEED/VEGETABLE OIL
1 TABLESPOON WHITE WINE VINEGAR
⅔ TABLESPOON DIJON MUSTARD
LEMON JUICE, TO TASTE
PINCH O' SALT

TO SERVE

• MILK BUNS OR SESAME
SEED BUNS
• SWISS/EDAM/HAVARTI
CHEESE (FOR MELTING)
• SHREDDED LETTUCE

GEAR

IN ORDER OF RAD
TO MORE
PAIN-IN-THE-ARSE:
FOOD PROCESSOR/
BLENDER/MORTAR
AND PESTLE

MAYO TIME! IF YOU WANNA GET THE FULL EXPERIENCE, YOU CAN MAKE THE MAYO YOURSELF OR YOU CAN JUST USE EGG MAYO THAT YOU BOUGHT IN A CYLINDRICAL GLASS THING ███████████ . . . I DARE NOT UTTER ITS NAME.

IF YOU DO WANNA MAKE IT, THEN IT'S SUPER QUICK. THIS IS HOW:

GRAB YOURSELF AN EMPTY SAUCEPAN (NO LID REQUIRED),

THROW A TEA TOWEL OVER IT LIKE A LID AND THEN PLACE A STAINLESS BOWL LARGER THAN THE POT ON TOP. THIS STOPS THE BOWL FUCKEN PISSING YOU OFF BY MOVING AROUND ALL OVER THE SHOP WHILE YOU'RE TRYING TO WHISK AND POUR AT THE SAME TIME. ███████

IN THAT BOWL GOES 1 EGG YOLK, WHISK IT UP.

NOW VERY FUCKEN SLOWLY (!!!) TIP IN THE GRAPESEED/VEGE OIL WHILE WHISKING WITH YOUR SPARE HAND. IF YOU ARE SLOW WITH IT YOU SHOULD SEE IT STARTING TO TURN INTO A MAYO-LOOKING MIXTURE. WHEN YOU GET THROUGH HALF THAT OIL, ADD IN THE VINEGAR AND GET BACK TO YOUR OIL TIPPING/WHISKING GIG. ███████

WATCH AS IT CHANGES COLOUR AS YOU WHISK AND SPIN OUT WONDERING HOW MAYO IS MADE OUT OF ONLY THAT SHIT. ONCE YOU HAVE SLOWLY ADDED THE REMAINING OIL, IN GOES THE TABLESPOON OF DIJON, A SQUEEZE OF LEMON JUICE AND A PINCH OF SALT, WHICH YOU WHISK ALL THROUGH. ONCE IT LOOKS LIKE THE CONSISTENCY OF MAYO, THEN IT PROBABLY IS. YOU CAN ADD MORE LEMON IF YOU LIKE IT MORE TART.

Honey mustard chicken is the most fucken relentlessly requested recipe on the channel and probably one of the most Defqon.1-level jar sauce abominations to ever hit the shelves. It's such rotten garbage that I went totally off that bastard of a sickly-sweet dish for years, but I'M BACK CHAMPIONS AND WE'VE FIXED IT! The idea is to help you escape any chance of having to eat that trash again. I've loved a bit of sweet and savoury action all the way back to an unhealthy obsession with Lemon Crisp biscuits as a kid. I actually did an advert for Pizza Shapes when I was eleven years old and I got paid in Lemon Crisp biscuits . . . Dad ate half of them, I think. Anyway, I'm getting a little off track here – this isn't a freaken recipe for biscuits, but it is one for sweet and savoury chicken radness.

SERVES:
4–6
COOKING TIME:
under an hour

HECTOMETER: 5/10

KEY:

Comfort Food | Feed the Team | Kiddo Friendly | Quick Sticks

INGREDIENTS

8 MEDIUM OR 6 LARGE SKIN-ON BONELESS CHICKEN THIGHS

SALT

1 TABLESPOON VEGETABLE OIL

25 G UNSALTED BUTTER

1 ONION, PEELED AND SLICED

1 SMALL BUNCH PARSLEY, STALKS AND LEAVES CHOPPED, BUT KEPT SEPARATE

6 GARLIC CLOVES, PEELED AND CHOPPED

1 TABLESPOON THYME LEAVES, CHOPPED

2 TABLESPOONS DIJON MUSTARD

2 TABLESPOONS WHOLEGRAIN MUSTARD

1½ TABLESPOONS HONEY

½ CUP WHITE WINE

1 CUP CHICKEN STOCK OR WATER

3 TEASPOONS PLAIN FLOUR

125 G CRÈME FRAÎCHE OR SOUR CREAM (FULL-FAT STUFF WORKS BEST)

Plonk!

Chicken Stock

SEEDY 'OL MUSTARD

SOUR CREAM

NOW YOU CAN OF COURSE DO THIS WITH CHICKEN BREAST BUT SINCE MAKING THE SHIFT TO CHICKEN THIGH, LIFE IN GENERAL HAS BECOME WAY BETTER. CHICKEN BREAST IS FINE AND ALL, BUT TAKES SOME WORK TO STOP IT FROM TASTING DRY AS A MOUTHFUL OF FUCKEN CHALK. SO LET'S CRACK ON WITH THE SKIN-ON THIGHS. SEASON THEM WITH SALT AND PLACE SKIN-SIDE DOWN INTO A ... WAIT FOR IT... COLD PAN! SOZ *WOT?* YEAH THAT'S RIGHT CHAMPION, A COLD PAN WITH A TABLESPOON OF OIL IN IT.

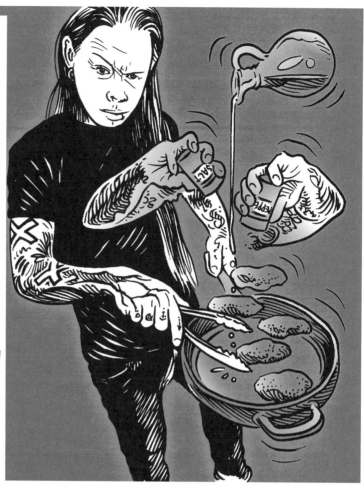

TURN ON THE STOVE TO A MEDIUM HEAT BUT **DON'T TOUCH** THE THIGHS.

WE WANT THEM TO STAY PUT FACE DOWN RENDERING IN THE OIL SO THEY GET SUPER CRISPY PANTS. KEEP THE HEAT AT MEDIUM UNTIL YOU HEAR IT STARTING TO SIZZLE ME TIMBERS, AND FROM THAT POINT IT'S 8 MINUTES UNTIL FLIP TIME.

ONCE THE SKIN SIDE IS GOLDEN BROWN TOWN, USE TONGS TO FLIP THEM OVER AND GIVE IT A HARD 5 ON THE OTHER SIDE (AT THE SAME HEAT).

PRESS THE CHICKEN THIGH EJECT BUTTON AND REMOVE FROM THE PAN AND REST ON A PLATE WHILE YOU CRACK ON WITH THE SAUCE.

INTO THE RECENTLY VACATED PAN, ADD YA BUTTER ON MEDIUM HEAT AGAIN. ONCE THAT SHIT HAS MELTED, FUCKEN BANG IN YA ONION AND CHOPPED-UP PARSLEY STALKS SANS LEAVES FOR 3-4 MINUTES UNTIL NICE AND SOFT. THEN IN WE GO WITH THE GARLIC AND THYME LEAVES AND COOK FOR ANOTHER 2 MINUTES.

MUSTARD BE ABOUT TIME TO PUT YA BLOODY MUSTARDZZZ IN THE PAN ALONG WITH THE HONEY, WINE AND STOCK AS YOU BRING IT EVER SO AWESOMELY TO A SIMMER, CHAMPION.

IN A BOWL BUNG IN YOUR FLOUR AND SPOON IN A LITTLE OF THE PAN JUICE THEN WHISK TOGETHER INTO A PASTE-LIKE CONSISTENCY. NOW BACK INTO THE PAN WITH YOUR MAGICAL CHICKEN FLOUR PASTE ALONG WITH THE CRÈME FRAÎCHE OR SOUR CREAM AND COOK FOR A FEW MINUTES.

CRÈME FRAÎCHE

OMG WHAT THE FUCK IS THIS CHICKEN STILL DOING ON A FUCKEN PLATE RIGHT NOW? ALL GOOD, LET'S FIX THAT WAGON AND BUNG IT BACK INTO THE MUSTARDY CREAMY NON JAR-EY GOODNESS WITH THE CHICKEN SKIN FACING UP SO THE SAUCE DOESN'T KILL ALL THAT CRISPY HARD WORK. GIVE IT AROUND 5 MINUTES IN THE SAUCE THERE BOSS; WE WANNA HEAT IT UP GOOD.

UNDERCOOKED CHICKEN IS A NOT-SO-FUN RIDE ON A SLIPPERY SLIDE TO BAD NEWS, SO MAKE SURE IT'S HEATED THROUGH.

THE (CHICKEN) WINGS OF LOVE ♡

Let's not kid ourselves here, wings are clearly the best part of the chicken. But something magical happens when you go and make them so much more awesome by covering them in rad stuff and deep frying them to a point where you're almost concerned with how many of these fucken things you could probably put away in one sitting. This dish also gives us a chance to make chipotle mayo together, which is very trendy indeed and also super fucken tasty. So drop kick that zinger and let's make a winner.

SERVES:
4–6
COOKING TIME:
1.5 hours,
including marinating

HECTOMETER: 6/10

KEY:
Cheap AF | Comfort Food | Kiddo Friendly | Side Mission

INGREDIENTS

- I TABLESPOON GARLIC POWDER
- I TABLESPOON GROUND WHITE PEPPER
- I TABLESPOON ONION POWDER
- I ½ TABLESPOONS SWEET SMOKED PAPRIKA
- 2 TEASPOONS CAYENNE PEPPER
- 2 TEASPOONS DRIED THYME OR DRIED OREGANO
- I TABLESPOON SALT FLAKES
- 600 ML BUTTERMILK
- 1.2 KG CHICKEN WINGS
- 2½ CUPS PLAIN FLOUR
- ½ CUP CORNFLOUR
- ENOUGH VEGETABLE OIL TO HALF FILL A DEEP
  SAUCEPAN (I L OR POSSIBLY MORE), TO DEEP FRY

CHIPOTLE MAYO

- 300 ML VEGETABLE OIL
- 2 TEASPOONS DIJON MUSTARD
- I GARLIC CLOVE, CHOPPED
- I TABLESPOON FINELY CHOPPED CHIPOTLE
  IN ADOBO (FROM A TIN), OR
  2 TEASPOONS CHIPOTLE POWDER
- I LIME, ZESTED AND JUICED, PLUS EXTRA
- LIME WEDGES, TO SERVE
- I EGG, AT ROOM TEMPERATURE
- SALT, TO TASTE

BEFORE WE KICK OFF THE CHICKEN WINGS BIT I SHOULD REMIND YOU THAT THESE MEASUREMENTS ARE AUSTRALIAN STANDARD MEASUREMENTS, SO I TABLESPOON IS A 20ML AND NOT A 15ML MEASURE LIKE SOME OTHER PARTS OF THE WORLD.

WE MUST LOVE BIG TABLESPOONS HERE OR SOMETHING! SO WITH THAT SAID, GET YOUR MASSIVE 20ML TABLESPOON FROM WHAT I'M SURE IS AN ENORMOUS CUTLERY DRAWER AND COMBINE THE SPICES TOGETHER IN A SMALL BOWL WITH THE SALT.

NOW REMOVE 2 TABLESPOONS OF THE SPICE MIX YOU JUST MADE AND PUT THEM INTO A BIG BOWL WITH THE BUTTERMILK. STIR TOGETHER TO COMBINE.

20ML TBS

SALT

YOU'RE GONNA NEED A SHITLOAD OF OIL FOR THIS 'CAUSE WE ARE DEEP FRYING, SO SO2 ABOUT IT.

GET YOURSELF A LARGE SAUCEPAN OR YOUR DEEPEST PAN AND HALF-FILL WITH OIL, WHICH IS PROBABLY A SHITLOAD DEPENDING ON THE SIZE OF YOUR PAN. WE WANNA BRING THIS TO THE PRETTY SPECIFIC TEMPERATURE OF BETWEEN 150 AND 160°C.

WARNING!
IF YOU JUST KEEP HEATING THE FUCKEN OIL TEMPERATURE THROUGH THE ROOF, THE SHIT MIGHT BURST INTO FUCKEN FLAMES, AND BURNING OIL IS A REAL 'BURN YOUR HOUSE DOWN' VIBE, SO HAVING A THERMOMETER AROUND IS A SICK MOVE TO AVOID THIS PALAVER.

150 - 160°C

I USE A MEAT THERMOMETER THAT CAN HANDLE HEATS UP TO THIS EXTREME AND I RECOMMEND YOU USE A THERMOMETER THAT SUITS THE JOB IF YOU WANNA PLAY IT SAFE.

MONITOR THE OIL TEMP THE WHOLE WAY THROUGH THE COOKING PROCESS AND TRY YOUR BEST TO KEEP IT AT AROUND THE 150-160°C MARK.

SURF $TURF MIE GORENG

There's not a person I know who hasn't smashed the absolute shit out of a metric fuck-tonne of mie goreng packets in their time. Whether I've been dragging the bottom of the drawer for change to sort a feed, coming home hungry and late drunk af, or even just being up for a trusty, spicy, instant noodle kick in the arse, instant mie goreng has been there for my younger self in times when I've been stuck in a real jam. This might sound a touch contradictory to my whole 'fuck packet food' rhetoric, but I gotta pay tribute to this absolute institution of an instant meal and cook one that will hopefully make you shit yourself with excitement, and not because you regretted eating the third packet of instant ones for dinner three nights in a row.

SERVES:
4
COOKING TIME:
30 mins–1 hour

HECTOMETER: 5/10

KEY:
Low Stress | Quick Sticks

INGREDIENTS

250 G SHELLED AND CLEANED RAW PRAWNS
(FROM ABOUT 500 G SHELL-ON PRAWNS)
500 G BONELESS CHICKEN THIGH FILLETS
4 SPRING ONIONS
6 GARLIC CLOVES, PEELED AND FINELY CHOPPED
2 TABLESPOONS VEGETABLE OIL
1½ CUPS THINLY SLICED WHITE CABBAGE
1½–2 TABLESPOONS SAMBAL OELEK OR 2-3 TABLESPOONS SRIRACHA
1/3 CUP KECAP MANIS
JUICE OF 1 LIME PLUS 4 WEDGES, TO SERVE
1 TABLESPOON SOY SAUCE
1 TEASPOON SESAME OIL
400 G COOKED EGG NOODLES (LIKE HOKKIEN)
100 G BEAN SPROUTS
4 EGGS
CRISPY FRIED ONIONS AND THINLY SLICED RED CHILLI, TO SERVE

IF YOU BOUGHT PRAWNS STILL IN THEIR SHELLS - HOPEFULLY NICE ONES - THEN NOW IS A RIPPER TIME TO PEEL, CLEAN (SLICE DOWN THEIR BACK AFTER PEELING AND REMOVE THE POOP TUBE) AND SET THEM ASIDE.

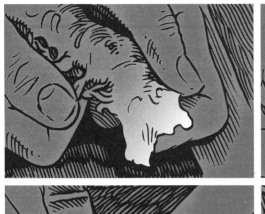

DICE YOUR SKINLESS CHICKEN THIGHS INTO 2-CM WIDE STRIPS OR CHUNKS OR FUCKEN WHATEVER YA BLOODY WANT REALLY.

THINLY SLICE YOUR SPRING ONIONS, SETTING A PINCH ASIDE TO SERVE AT THE END. THE REST CAN GO IN A BOWL CHOPPED UP WITH YOUR GARLIC.

IF YOU HAVE A WOK, THIS IS A SICK BIT OF KIT FOR THIS GIG SO GRAB IT AND FANG IT ON THE STOVE, ADD THE OIL AND CRANK THE HEAT TO HIGH. (YOUR BIGGEST FRYING PAN IS THE NEXT BEST THING.)

AWAY WE GO IN WITH THE CHICKEN THIGHS TO STIR FRY FOR 4-5 MINUTES TILL BROWNED. WHAT DO YA KNOW, JACK, IT'S TIME TO ADD THAT SURF (PRAWNS) TO THE TURF (CHOOK) ALONG WITH THE SPRING ONIONS AND GARLIC. TOSS THIS LOT AROUND FOR A COUPLE OF MINUTES.

CEVICHE ON THE BEACH, EH?

One of the most beautiful things in life is the simplicity of friendship. Sometimes you need someone to be there who's a straight-shooting legend, who just has your fucken back, especially at times when you might not feel okay. This ceviche recipe is inspired by one such moment, when my two best mates and I formed a mighty trio of untouchable togetherness! We set a goal to have a fucken shit-hot pool party up north, eat some good food and get through the tough times together. Ceviche is something that cemented the memory of that time together for me – I remember us all being amazed at how such a simple dish worked such fucken magic and took some of the worry away for just a moment. Times are tough, maybe we all just need to have ceviche on the beach, eh?

SERVES:
2–3
COOKING TIME:
less than 30 mins

HECTOMETER: 2/10

KEY:
Feed the Team | Low Stress | Quick Sticks | Side Mission

INGREDIENTS

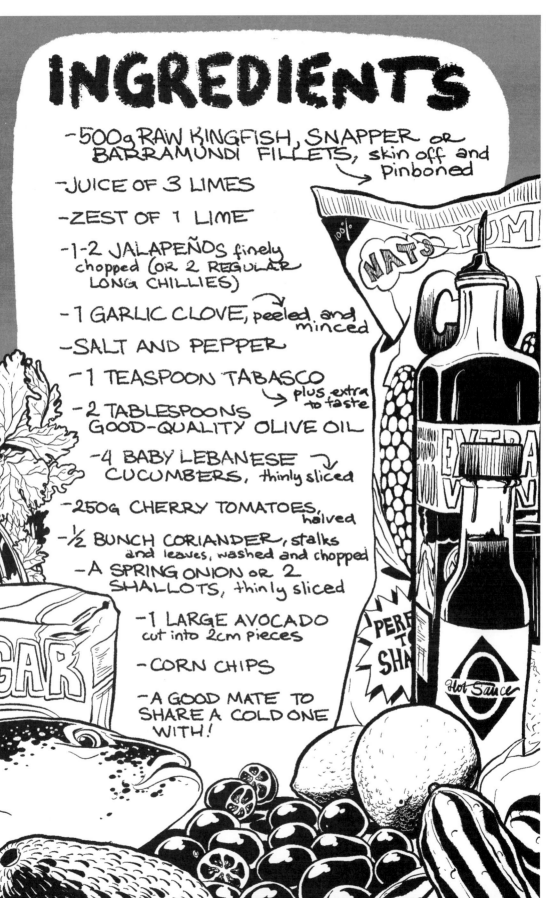

- 500g RAW KINGFISH, SNAPPER or BARRAMUNDI FILLETS, skin off and pinboned

- JUICE OF 3 LIMES

- ZEST OF 1 LIME

- 1-2 JALAPEÑOS finely chopped (OR 2 REGULAR LONG CHILLIES)

- 1 GARLIC CLOVE, peeled and minced

- SALT AND PEPPER

- 1 TEASPOON TABASCO
  plus extra to taste

- 2 TABLESPOONS GOOD-QUALITY OLIVE OIL

- 4 BABY LEBANESE CUCUMBERS, thinly sliced

- 250g CHERRY TOMATOES, halved

- ½ BUNCH CORIANDER, stalks and leaves, washed and chopped

- A SPRING ONION or 2 SHALLOTS, thinly sliced

- 1 LARGE AVOCADO cut into 2cm pieces

- CORN CHIPS

- A GOOD MATE TO SHARE A COLD ONE WITH!

FIRSTLY, IT WOULD MAKE SENSE TO CHAT ABOUT THE FISH. THERE IS A LONG LIST OF FISH YOU CAN USE FOR THIS, BUT BY FAR MY FAVOURITE IS FRESH KINGFISH IF YOU CAN GET YOUR HANDS ON IT.

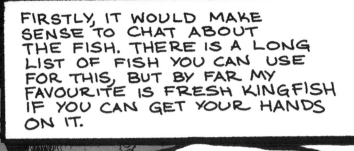

FISH LIST

-FRESH KINGFISH
-SNAPPER
-BARRAMUNDI

FROZEN FISH IS GONNA BE CONSIDERABLY LESS RAD SO FRESH AF SHOULD BE YOUR MOTTO HERE

-AVOC

MAKE SURE WHATEVER FISH YOU BUY HAS BEEN BONED THOROUGHLY. FISH BONES ARE A MASSIVE FUCKWIT TO MANAGE ON THEIR WAY DOWN THE OESOPHAGUS, SO GIVE THE FILLETS THE OLD ROBOCOP SCAN BEFORE YOU KICK OFF TO AVOID FURTHER LIFE STRESS.

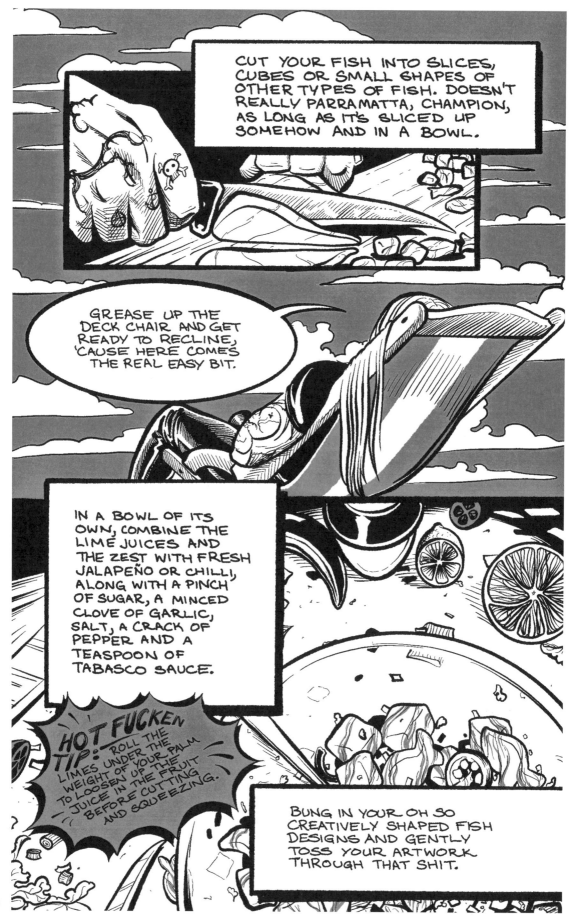

I MEAN, TO BE FAIR, YOU'RE 10-15 MINUTES AWAY FROM SLIDING INTO THE LAP OF EASYGOING LUXURY, SO LETS DO A FEW LAST THINGS TO SET OUR-SELVES UP FOR THE MOST POWERFULLY RELAXED SESH OF ALL TIME, AND MAKE THE REST OF IT.

IN A BOWL POUR YOUR OLIVE OIL.

ADD SLICED CUCUMBERS (AGAIN AT YOUR ARTISTIC DIRECTION, PICASSO),

ALONG WITH THE TOMATOES, CORIANDER AND SPRING ONIONS OR SHALLOTS.

That. IS. IT.

SERVE WITH SOME NON-COMMITAL CORN CHIPS AND A COLD BEER, MAYBE TALK SOME SHIT WITH A MATE AND TRY TO FORGET YOUR WORRIES JUST FOR A MINUTE.

IT'S BEAUTIFUL FOOD AND YOU'RE A BEAUTIFUL PERSON.

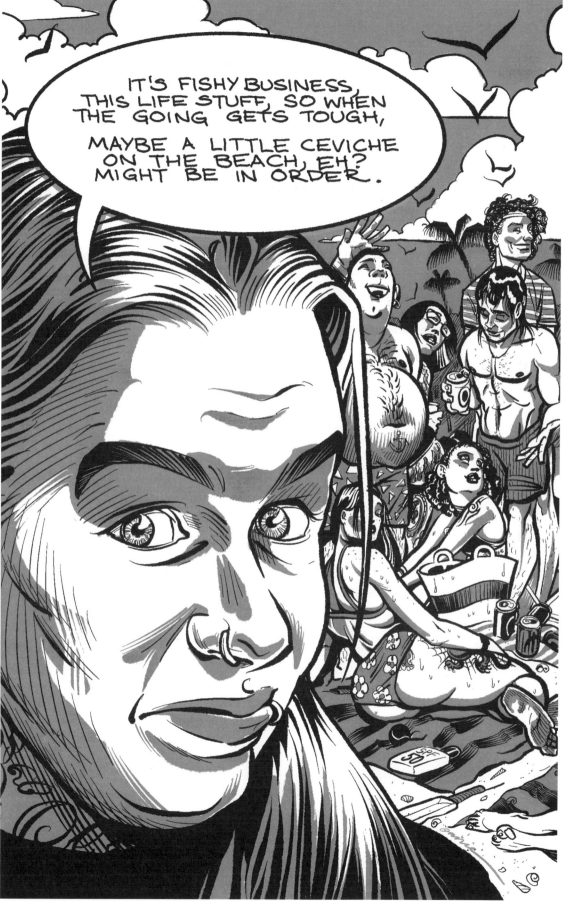

FISH CAKES

Just imagine it was everyone's birthday every day and you didn't have to go to work or school or deal with any fuckwits 'cause you're a fish as well, which is weird, but also cool 'cause you're also eternally at a pool party in the ocean . . . (*takes deep breath*) aaaaaand someone's made you a cake and you also made them a cake and they are both made out of fish, which again sounds weird at first, BUT fish sometimes eat other types of fish too, which is totally chill when you're a fish at a birthday party, and plus we are making your favourite kind of fish cake so whoo hooooooooooooo!

SERVES:

3–4

COOKING TIME:

about 1 hour*

* depending on whether you make your own curry paste and how staunch your blender/food processor is

HECTOMETER: 3–6*/10

KEY:

Low Stress | Quick Sticks | Side Mission

INGREDIENTS

500 G SKINLESS WHITE FISH FILLETS (LIKE BASA, LING OR
   BLUE-EYE TREVALLA), CHOPPED UP HEAPS AS
½ BUNCH CORIANDER (STALKS AND LEAVES),
   ROUGHLY CHOPPED
3 MAKRUT/LIME LEAVES, THINLY SLICED
2 TABLESPOONS FISH SAUCE
2 TEASPOONS BROWN SUGAR
2-3 TABLESPOONS RED CURRY PASTE
   (SEE SOUP RECIPE PAGE 288 TO MAKE YOUR OWN)
PINCH O' SALT
1 EGG
¼ CUP RICE FLOUR
2 TABLESPOONS FINELY GRATED GINGER
75 G GREEN BEANS
2 TABLESPOONS VEGETABLE OIL

CHILLI OR SWEET CHILLI SAUCE, EXTRA CORIANDER LEAVES
   AND LIME WEDGES, TO SERVE

INTO THE FOOD PROCESSOR GOES YOUR ALREADY CHOPPED UP FISH, MAKING SURE WHATEVER FISH YOU DO DECIDE TO USE IS OF COURSE BONELESS 'CAUSE A BONE CAKE IS GONNA END THE PARTY EARLY.

GIVE IT A QUICK RUN IN THERE TO MAKE THE FISH INTO A PASTE.

NOW, IN WITH THE FISH PASTE GOES THE CORIANDER ALONG WITH THE MAKRUT LIME LEAVES, FISH SAUCE, BROWN SUGAR,

RED CURRY PASTE, A PINCH OF SALT, THE EGG, THE RICE FLOUR AND YOUR GRATED GINGER.

NOW WHIZ IT ALL TOGETHER TILL IT'S SMOOTH.

FINELY CHOP UP YOUR GREEN BEANS AND STIR THEM THROUGH THE PASTE WITH A SPOON.

CREATE SOME FISHY BIRTHDAY RISSOLE-SHAPED LITTLE CAKES WITH ABOUT 1.5–2 TABLESPOONS OF MIXTURE AT A TIME.

WITH A LARGE SPOON OR YOUR HANDS,

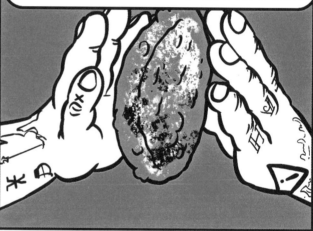

LAY THEM OUT ON BAKING PAPER AS YOU GO. THIS CAN BE TRICKY

DOLLOPING A BIT OF MIXTURE INTO THE OIL AND GENTLY SQUASHING THE CAKES FLAT CAN WORK TOO IF THE MIX IS TOO STICKY.

BUT DON'T FRET TOO MUCH IF THEY WON'T SET INTO PATTIES BEFORE YOU COOK THEM.

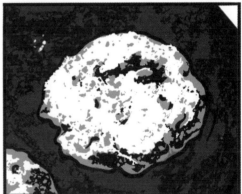

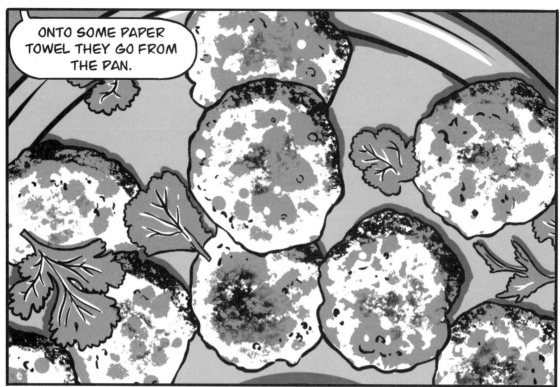

ZERO FUCKS MAC 'N' CHEESE

A →

C-60

100   50   0

STEREO

If you have any awareness of or give a fuck about calories, you may want to put your welding helmet on and take a deep breath for this doozy, champion. Food like this is so entirely ridiculous and fucked up – true food debauchery with an almost total disregard for healthy eating, but also pretty amazing.

Also . . . being 'healthy' can mean a lot of things depending on where you're standing in the room; joy is healthy too, just saying. This dish was requested on my social media so often it would be rude not to have a crack at this smash-hits calorific tidal wave.

So dust off the Bolton back catalogue, shit is about get cheesy.

SERVES:
4–6
COOKING TIME:
1–1½ hours

HECTOMETER: 5/10

KEY:
Comfort Food | Kiddo Friendly | Side Mission | Vego

INGREDIENTS

- 500 G MACARONI PASTA (OR ANY SHIT EXCEPT MAYBE LONG PASTA LIKE SPAGHETTI, LINGUINE ETC)
- 3-4 TABLESPOONS BUTTER, PLUS MORE FOR GREASING
- 150 G CHEDDAR CHEESE
- 150 G MOZZARELLA
- 1 BROWN ONION, PEELED
- WHOLE BULB OF GARLIC, PEELED AND DICED
- 1 L FULL-CREAM MILK
- 2 TABLESPOONS PLAIN FLOUR
- 100 G SHAVED PARMESAN
- 2 HEAPED TEASPOONS MUSTARD POWDER/ DIJON MUSTARD
- SALT AND PEPPER
- 1 TEASPOON PAPRIKA (OPTIONAL)
- 1/3 - 1 CUP PANKO BREADCRUMBS
- PINCH CHOPPED PARSLEY
- 1/2 TEASPOON DRIED THYME

LETS HAVE A MELTDOWN, SHALL WE?

PRE-HEAT THE OVEN TO 200°C FAN-FORCED (220°C CONVENTIONAL).

BOIL SOME WATER IN A LARGE POT ON THE STOVE, BANG IN SOME SALT AND **HALF-WAY** COOK YOUR PASTA...

...DRAIN IT.

RETURN TO THE PAN.

STIR THROUGH A TABLESPOON OF BUTTER AND SET ASIDE.

GRATE THE RESPECTIVE CHEESES INTO SEPARATE BOWLS.

AS FINELY AS YOU CAN BE BOTHERED, SLICE THE ONION AND BUNG IN A BOWL, FOLLOWED BY YOUR DICED GARLIC.

POUR A LITRE OF MILK INTO A SMALL POT

AND GENTLY WARM IT UP (NOT BOIL) ON THE STOVE.

Spinach and ricotta pie can get a bit fucking samey and boring if you don't add a little something to it. That little something is feta, 'cause feta in it is better. It's an all-time sterling winner, this one. If you're trying to watch ya waistline, Warren, then you can sub for low-fat ricotta and crank up the spinach amount, Popeye. Whatever you go for, it's better for ya than a servo pie.

SERVES:
6
COOKING TIME:
45 mins–1 hour

HECTOMETER: 4/10

KEY:
Comfort Food | Feed the Team | Impress the Judges |
Quick Sticks | Vego

INGREDIENTS

1 BROWN ONION
6 CLOVES GARLIC
8 SPRING ONIONS
500 G ENGLISH SPINACH, WASHED
4-5 TABLESPOONS OLIVE OIL, PLUS EXTRA FOR GREASING
25 G BUTTER, PLUS OPTIONAL EXTRA FOR GREASING
650 G RICOTTA
150 G FETA, CRUMBLED
1 TEASPOON GROUND NUTMEG
SALT
PEPPER
2 EGGS

10 SHEETS FILO PASTRY,
DEFROSTED IF FROZEN,
OR EVEN BETTER
– USE FRESH STUFF

GEAR YA NEED:
25-30 CM PIE DISH
OR BAKING TRAY
PASTRY BRUSH

HERE COMES THE TRICKIER PART:

THE FILO PASTRY BIT. GRAB YOURSELF A PIE DISH IF YOU HAVE ONE, OTHERWISE A ROASTING TRAY THAT'S AN INCH OR TWO DEEP WILL DO.

GREASE IT UP WITH OLIVE OIL AND PLACE ON A SINGLE SHEET OF FILO SO THAT HALF OF IT HANGS OFF THE EDGE. USING THE PASTRY BRUSH, YOU'LL WANNA LIGHTLY BRUSH ON SOME OIL TO THE FIRST PIECE OF FILO THAT'S ON THE INSIDE OF THE DISH.

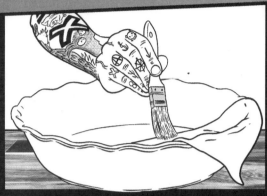

NEXT LAY ON ANOTHER SHEET IN THE SAME FASHION BUT IMAGINE IT LIKE THIS: YOU WANT TO ARRANGE THEM IN A WAY SO THAT THERE IS HALF A SHEET'S WORTH OF FILO HANGING OFF EVERY SIDE AND CORNER OF THE DISH.

IF YOU'VE GOT A ROUND DISH THEN THE OVERHANGING PASTRY WILL FORM A SUNSHINE KIND OF SHAPE.

THE REASON IS THAT ONCE YOU'VE ADDED THE FILLING YOU'LL FLAP THOSE BITS ON TOP TO MAKE A LID.

REPEAT WITH THE REMAINING SHEETS, BRUSHING ON YOUR OIL AND OVERLAPPING AS YOU GO UNTIL YOU'VE COME THE WHOLE WAY AROUND YOUR DISH.

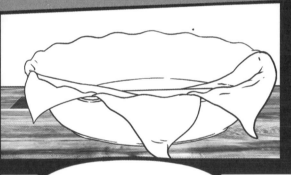

CUT IT UP AND SERVE TO YOUR FAVOURITE CHAMPIONS.
WHAT A RIPPER BEAUTY.
BUNKWAA

SPICY PANTS SHAKSHUKA
(BUSH DOOF RESCUE)

Shakshuka is one of those fucken brekkie all-timers. Whether you're trying to impress someone with your seemingly wild 'dinner for breakfast' moves, or blow the minds of your hungover mates at a bush doof with this one-pan wonder, shakkas has got the lot. Seriously, you can even make this on a camp stove rather than eating another load of punishingly over-spiced curry out of a paper bowl. Don't do that . . . do this.

SERVES:
3–4
COOKING TIME:
30–40 mins

HECTOMETER: 3/10

KEY:
Cheap AF | Quick Sticks | Vego

INGREDIENTS
1 RED ONION
1 RED CAPSICUM
1 BUNCH CORIANDER OR PARSLEY,
WASHED AND DRIED
1-2 RED CHILLIES, HALVED AND DESEEDED
4+ GARLIC CLOVES (GO ON, BANG IN A WHOLE FUCKEN GARLIC BULB)
3 TABLESPOONS EXTRA-VIRGIN OLIVE OIL
1 TEASPOON CUMIN SEEDS
½ - 1 TEASPOON HOT PAPRIKA
1 TEASPOON CAYENNE PEPPER
2 TINS WHOLE PEELED TOMATOES (NOT SHIT ONES)
1 TEASPOON BROWN SUGAR
SALT & PEPPER, TO TASTE
4-6 EGGS
100G CRUMBLED FETA AND TRENDY TOAST, TO SERVE

RIGHTY'O JOE.

PEEL AND DICE THE RED ONION, DE-SEED THE CAPSICUM, DICE IT UP AND BANG ALL THAT SHIT IN A BOWL TOGETHER.

GRAB A BUNCH OF CORIANDER (OR PARSLEY IF YOU HATE CORIANDER, YA WEIRDO), CUT THE HAIRY ARSE OFF IT, THEN ROUGHLY CUT THE STALK PART AWAY FROM THE FOLIAGE PART UP THE TOP. KEEP THE LEAFY BIT ASIDE AND CHOP THE STALKS UP (THAT'S RIGHT, CHOP THE STALKS) AND BANG THEM IN THE SAME BOWL AS THE ONIONS AND CAPSICUM.

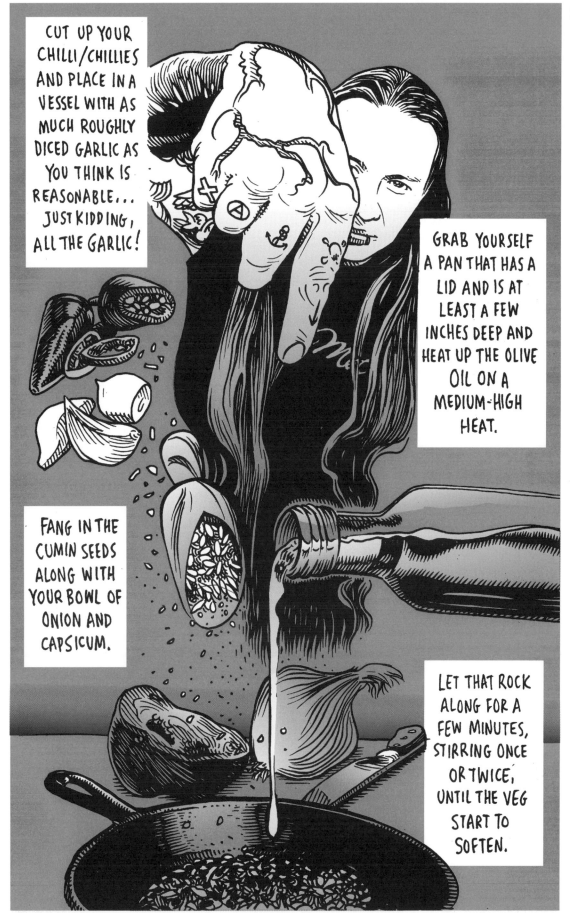

THEN COMES THE BIT THAT ALWAYS MAKES EVERYONE SAY THAT CLICHÉ, 'WOW THAT SMELLS AMAZING, WHAT ARE YOUUUUU COOOOKIIINNNNGGG?' TO WHICH YOU CAN REPLY... AGAIN, 'OH, THAT'S PROBABLY THE GARLIC' BECAUSE AT THIS POINT YOU WILL HAVE ADDED YOUR GARLIC AND CHILLI TO THE PAN, AND THAT'S GREAT 'CAUSE WE NEED TO COOK THAT NOW, AS WELL AS THE PAPRIKA AND CAYENNE. GIVE IT ALL A STIR AND COOK FOR A MINUTE OR TWO.

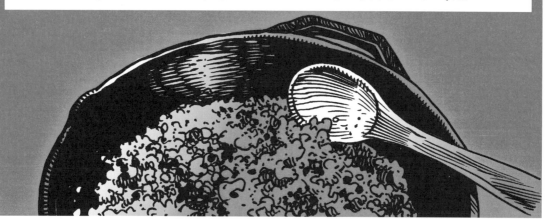

INTO THE PAN GO YOUR TINS OF WHOLE TOMATOES, BREAKING THEM APART WITH A WOODEN SPOON LIKE A COUPLE OF HIPPIE TOURISTS ARGUING OVER WHETHER BYRON BAY HAS SOLD OUT TO THE POINT OF BEING UNCOOL NOW. HALF-FILL ONE OF THE EMPTIED TOMATO CANS WITH WATER AND THEN, ODDLY ENOUGH, TIP THAT INTO THE OTHER EMPTY TIN, THEREFORE RINSING BOTH OF THEIR REMAINING TOMATOEYNESS TOGETHER AS YOU TIP ALL THAT PRATTLE-ON INTO THE PAN AS WELL.

FLICK IN A TEASPOON OF BROWN SUGAR ALONG WITH A PINCH OF SALT AND A CRACK OF PEPPER. TRY NOT TO GO TOO HARD ON THE SALT, 'CAUSE THERE'S NO COMING DOWN OFF THAT HIGH EASILY.

TURN THE HEAT RIGHT DOWN AND SIMMER SIMMER YA BIG WINNER FOR 15 MINUTES, OR ENOUGH TIME TO PUMP OUT A CUPPLA EYE-WATERINGLY BAD BEN HARPER COVERS ON THE MELODEON, LIKELY WITH SOME GUITAR-TAPPING ARSEHOLE CALLED WISH WHO CAN'T DECIDE WHETHER HE'S A GUITARIST, SHIT DRUMMER OR ASCENDING TO ANOTHER DIMENSION FULL OF ANNOYING FUCKWITS LIKE HIM.

AFTER THAT WHOLE SCENE HAS ENDED, BUNG 4-6 DING-HOLES INTO THE SAUCE AND CRACK YA EGGS DIRECTLY INTO THEM, SO THE THICKENED SAUCE STOPS THE EGG FROM RUNNING EVERYWHERE.

COOK THAT FOR ANOTHER 10 MINUTES ON LOW WITH A LID ON IT UNTIL THE EGGS ARE COOKED, OR BETTER YET – IF YOU HAPPEN TO BE AT A PLACE OF RESIDENCE THAT HAS BOTH A SHOWER AND A FUCKEN OVEN – CRANK THE OVEN TO 200°C FAN-FORCED (OR 220°C NON FANINATED), FANG IT IN THAT SHIT INSTEAD FOR 10 AND GO HAVE A SHOWER AND TAKE A LONG HARD LOOK AT YOURSELF, YA PEST.

ONCE THE EGGS LOOK FUCKEN COOKED ENOUGH FOR YOUR COOKED HEAD, THROW A BIT OF THE LEFTOVER CORIANDER/PARSLEY LEAVES OVER IT WITH SOME FETA, SERVE IT WITH SOME TRENDY SOURDOUGH TOAST OR JUST FUCKEN BREAD. FUCK IT, EVEN SLAM ON A BIT OF HOT SAUCE IF YOU'RE NOT SCARED OF ANOTHER VISIT TO THAT HARROWING COMPOSTING TOILET FULL OF SAWDUST, SHAME AND BAD MEMORIES UP ON THE HILL.

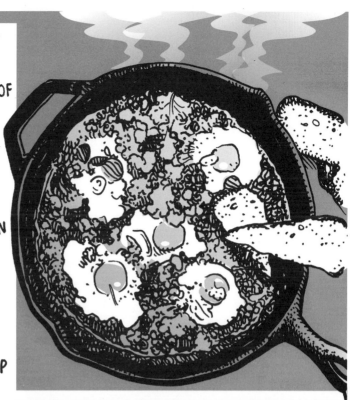

A DISH SO GOOD IT WILL EVEN OFFER YOUR SHATTERED ARSE A RIDE HOME FROM THE DOOF.

THE CURE

(not the band)

A
C-60

STEREO

Traditionally when you get sick as a dog, you go for soup, don't ya? So let's eat some fucking soup, legends. In my humble opinion, the best part about a pumpkin soup is the sweet potato and tonne of garlic that you put in it. I've never been a massive fan of pumpkin soup on its own if I'm to be honest: I reckon it lacks a bit of biff. In this version, the sweet potato high-fives the pumpkin in the best way, trust me.

SERVES:
8
COOKING TIME:
an hour and a bit
(depends how fast you are)

HECTOMETER: 4/10

KEY:
Cheap AF | Feed the Team | Vego

750 G SWEET POTATO
750 G BUTTERNUT PUMPKIN (NICE AND RIPE), DESEEDED
2 LEEKS
1 METAPHORICAL TONNE OF GARLIC (OR 1 WHOLE BULB)
1 LARGE BROWN ONION
2 RED CHILLIES (OPTIONAL)
ABOUT 2.5 CM THUMB FRESH GINGER
2 TABLESPOONS BUTTER
½ TEASPOON OF GROUND NUTMEG
5 CUPS CHICKEN OR VEGGIE STOCK
SALT
SOUR CREAM OR GREEK YOGURT, TO SERVE
PEPPER
CORIANDER, TO SERVE

GEAR YOU'LL NEED:

STICK BLENDER

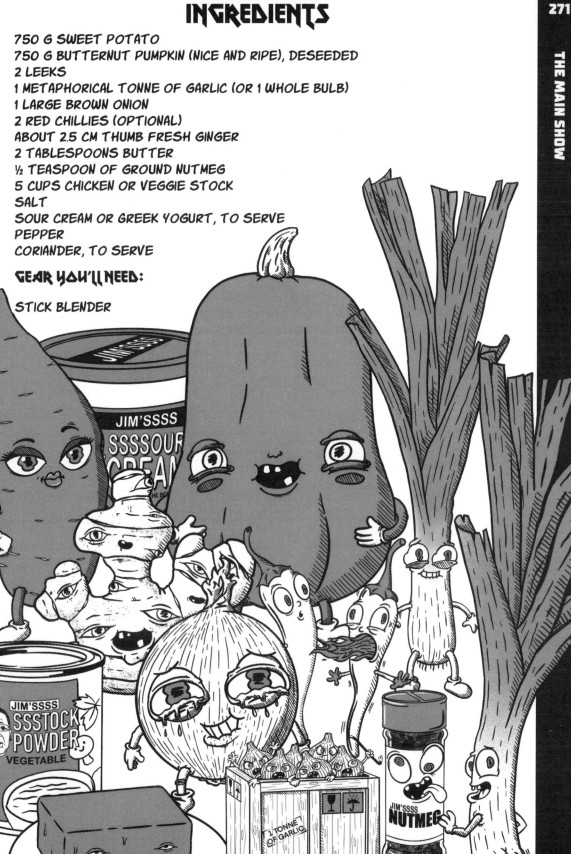

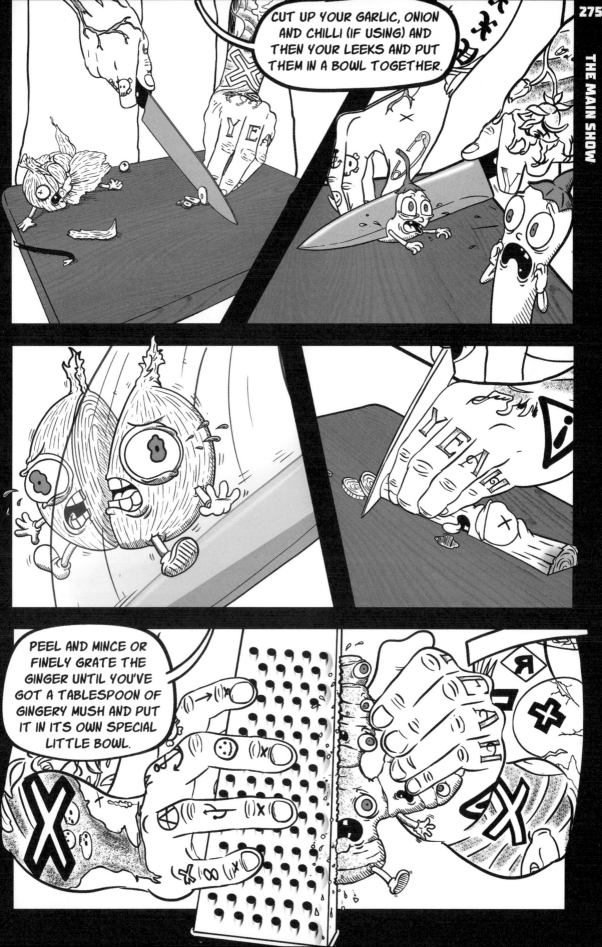

ADD A GOOD PINCH OF SALT, A LITTLE AT A TIME UNTIL IT TASTES THE AMOUNT OF SALTY THAT YOU'RE UP FOR.

SERVE IT UP WITH A GOOD BLOB OF GREEK YOGURT OR SOUR CREAM IN THE CENTRE WITH A CRACK OF PEPPER

AND CORIANDER IF IT DOESN'T TASTE LIKE FUCKEN SOAP TO YOU.

JIM'SSSS SSSSOUR CREAM

SSSSIMPLY THE BEST

AUSSSTRA MADE 600ml

THAT'S MORE OR LESS FUCKING IT, EASY AS YA LIKE.

THERE YOU HAVE IT CHAMPION, THE CURE TO WHAT AILS YA.

CHILLI, PUMPKIN & MUSHROOM RHYS-OTTO

(Dedicated to Rhys the chilli champion)

My mate Rhys loves chilli to a level that is almost scary, so I dedicate this dish to him, being that he was the only one who enjoyed it when I made it too hot. I accidentally made this so chilli once that I couldn't fucken eat it, so watch it on the spice there, tough guy. Now you can make it as chilli as ya fucken like, just adjust the level of heat as much as you need. Treat it like an artwork, but I recommend not adding too many layers of paint to said artwork, or you might kill it.

SERVES:
4–5
COOKING TIME:
about 45 mins–1 hour

HECTOMETER: 4/10

KEY:
Cheap AF | Quick Sticks | Vego

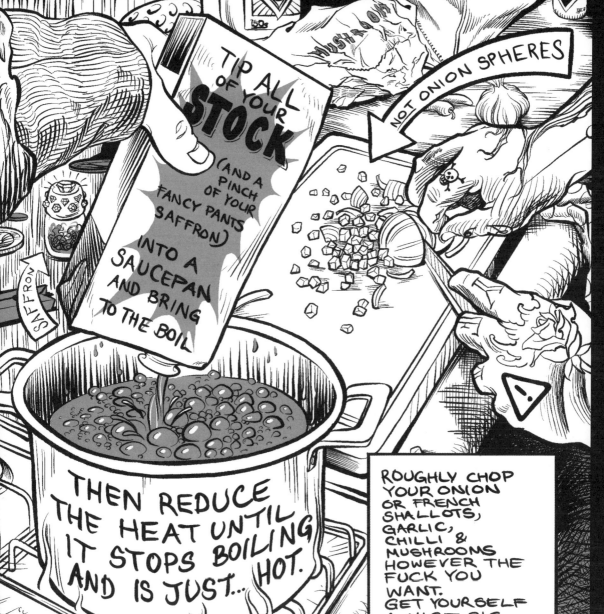

NOT ONION SPHERES

TIP ALL OF YOUR **STOCK** (AND A PINCH OF YOUR FANCY PANTS SAFFRON) INTO A SAUCEPAN AND BRING TO THE BOIL

SAFFRON

THEN REDUCE THE HEAT UNTIL IT STOPS BOILING AND IS JUST... HOT.

ROUGHLY CHOP YOUR ONION OR FRENCH SHALLOTS, GARLIC, CHILLI & MUSHROOMS HOWEVER THE FUCK YOU WANT. GET YOURSELF A NICE BIG FLAT-BOTTOMED PAN WITH DEEP SIDES.

FRY YOUR ONION, GARLIC, CHILLI & MUSHROOMS IN A KNOB OF BUTTER UNTIL THEY'RE SOFT.

JUST DON'T FUCKING BURN THEM. AN EASY WAY TO NOT BURN SOMETHING IS NOT TO TURN THE HEAT UP TO 1000.

FROM THERE YOU WANT TO ADD THE STOCK ONE LADLE AT A TIME AND FRY IT OFF. THIS SHIT IS FUCKING EASY: ALL YOU HAVE TO DO IS KEEP ADDING STOCK AND STIRRING 'TIL YOUR ARM FALLS OFF... OR UNTIL THE RICE IS COOKED.

THE WAY TO KNOW WHEN THE RICE IS COOKED IS BECAUSE IT FUCKING TASTES COOKED. I KNOW YOU'VE HAD RICE BEFORE SO DON'T PRETEND YOU DON'T KNOW WHAT THE FUCK COOKED RICE TASTES LIKE.
IF YOU WANT YOUR RICE SOFTER, ADD MORE STOCK. YOU LIKE YOUR RICE FIRMER? THEN ADD LESS STOCK

...DUH!

6:66
THE # OF THE BEAST

WAKE

BAKE

SERVE IT ON A PLATE,
A FRISBEE,
A FUCKING COMPACT DISC
OR WHATEVER YOU WANT
TO EAT IT ON

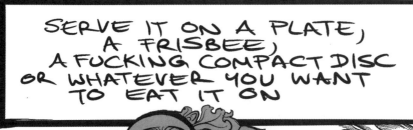

SPRINKLE OVER CHOPPED PARSLEY

WITH ADDITIONAL PARMESAN

AND A DRIZZLE OF OLIVE OIL
ON TOP UNLESS IT'S SHIT
OLIVE OIL — THEN DON'T PUT
THAT ON.

TOTAL WINNER DISH AND
EASY AS ALL GET OUT!

RED CURRY SWEET POTATO SOUP

I reckon sweet potato and red curry are two good mates just waiting to hang out. Imagine you were eating an amazingly silky, sweet but savoury soup that was also kind of a Thai curry flavour . . . Sounds wild, is rad. Let's do it!

SERVES:
3–4
COOKING TIME:
about 1 hour*
* if you make the curry paste

HECTOMETER: 6.5/10*

KEY:
Quick Sticks │ Side Mission │ Worth the Effort

CURRY PASTE INGREDIENTS

- 6 DRIED CHILLIES, SOAKED IN HOT WATER FOR 20 MINUTES, DRAINED
- 1 TEASPOON CUMIN SEEDS
- 1 TEASPOON CORIANDER SEEDS
- 1 TEASPOON BLACK PEPPERCORNS
- ROOTS FROM 1 BUNCH CORIANDER, WASHED (RESERVE STALKS AND LEAVES FOR SOUP)
- 1 TABLESPOON MINCED GALANGAL (OR GINGER)
- 4 FRESH LONG RED CHILLIES, PLUS EXTRA SLICES, TO SERVE
- 1 STALK LEMONGRASS, WHITE AND TENDER PART ONLY, ROUGHLY CHOPPED
- 2 MAKRUT LIME LEAVES
- 4 GARLIC CLOVES, PEELED
- 1½ TEASPOONS SHRIMP PASTE (OR 1 TABLESPOON FISH SAUCE)
- 2 SMALL RED ESCHALLOTS, PEELED AND ROUGHLY CHOPPED

SOUP INGREDIENTS

- 1 ONION
- A WHOLE BULB OF GARLIC
- 1 LEEK
- 800 G SWEET POTATO, PEELED AND CUT INTO 3CM PIECES
- 400 G BUTTERNUT PUMPKIN, PEELED AND CUT INTO 3CM PIECES
- 2 TABLESPOONS VEGETABLE OIL
- $\frac{1}{3}$–$\frac{1}{2}$ CUP RED CURRY PASTE
- 1 LITRE VEGETABLE OR CHICKEN STOCK
- 400 ML COCONUT MILK
- 1 LIME, JUICED
- CRISPY DRIED ONION TO SERVE

I S'POSE BEFORE WE MAKE ANY SOUPY MOVES HERE WE SHOULD GET THIS RED CURRY PASTE SORTED. YOU CAN OF COURSE USE PRE-MADE STUFF, BUT WHERE IS THE FUN IN THAT?

RIGHT-YO!

FUN IT IS.

IF YOU HAVEN'T GOT YOUR DRIED CHILLI ON THE SOAK YET, THEN AWAY YA GO WITH THAT.

THEN, OVER A MEDIUM HEAT GOES A SMALL FRYING PAN WITHOUT ANY OIL (NO OIL EVEN). DRY ROAST, AKA KICK ABOUT IN THE DRY PAN, YOUR CUMIN AND CORIANDER SEEDS ALONG WITH YOUR PEPPERCORNS FOR 2 MINUTES OR UNTIL FRAGRANT.

FUCK IT'S HOT!

MED

2 MIN

NO OIL EVEN

REMOVE FROM THE HEAT AND LET THEM COOL DOWN FOR A SECOND SIMON, THEN TIP INTO A MORTAR AND PESTLE OR A SMALL FOOD PROCESSOR/SPICE GRINDER TO BASH THAT LOT TOGETHER INTO A DUSTY CONSISTENCY.

NOW, IN THE INGREDIENTS LIST YOU MAY HAVE NOTICED THIS NEXT TO THE CORIANDER: '(RESERVE STALKS AND LEAVES FOR SOUP):'

LEAVES

THIS MEANS YOU SEPARATE THE CORIANDER INTO THREE PARTS, REALLY-THE ROOTS BEING THE ... WELL, ROOT BITS; THE MIDDLE THE STALK BITS THAT YOU SHOULD ROUGHLY CHOP; AND OF COURSE THE LEAVES BIT ARE ANOTHER THING ALTOGETHER.

STEMS

ROOTS

SET ASIDE THE STALKS AND LEAVES IN THEIR OWN SPECIAL BOWLS FOR LATER AND GET READY TO FANG THE ROOTS INTO THE MIX.

INTO THE FOOD PROCESSOR BOWL NEEDS TO BE THE SPICE MIX YOU JUST MADE, THE CORIANDER ROOTS AND EVERYTHING ELSE ON THE CURRY PASTE LIST. ADD A COUPLE OF TABLESPOONS OF WATER AND BLEND IT LIKE BECKHAM.

THERE WILL BE ENOUGH PASTE HERE TO HANG ONTO SOME IN YOUR FRIDGE (FOR A WEEK) OR FREEZER (FOR LONGER). WE ARE MOST CERTAINLY NOT GONNA USE ALL OF THAT SPICE IN THE SOUP OTHERWISE YOU MAY BLOW YOUR HEAD CLEAN OFF YOUR SHOULDERS WITH FLAVOUR.

LET'S RIP INTO IT.

HEAT THE OIL IN A LARGE SAUCEPAN OVER MEDIUM-HIGH HEAT, THEN IN GOES THE GARLIC, ONION AND LEEK AND THE RESERVED CHOPPED-UP CORIANDER STALKS, AND COOK FOR A FEW MINUTES UNTIL SOFTENED.

IN WITH ⅓ - ½ CUP OF YA RED CURRY PASTE AND COOK THAT OFF IN THE PAN FOR ANOTHER FEW MINUTES. BUNG IN THE SWEET POTATO AND PUMPKIN AND STIR FOR ANOTHER FEW MINUTES.

POUR IN THE STOCK, BRING TO THE BOIL THEN REDUCE THE HEAT AND COOK FOR 30 MINUTES OR UNTIL TENDER AS A GENTLE WANDER THROUGH THE BOTANICAL GARDENS READING RUMI TO A LOVER.

VEGENATOR 2

A →

C-60

JUDGEMENT TRAY LASAGNE

'My mission is to protect you' from shitty lasagne.
The amazing stuff that can go into a veggie lasagne is
fucken awesome – I occasionally prefer a good veg one over
a meat version because of all the amazing layers of flavours
you can get going on. This dish is layer upon layer of action-
packed radness. So let's get terminating our hunger and
prepare for Vegenator 2: Judgement Tray.

SERVES:
6–8
COOKING TIME:
coupla hours

HECTOMETER: 6/10

KEY:
Feed the Team │ Impress the Judges │ Kiddo Friendly │ Vego

INGREDIENTS

800 G - 1 KG BUTTERNUT PUMPKIN
2 TABLESPOONS OLIVE OIL
SALT
PEPPER
1 TEASPOON CHILLI FLAKES
2 TEASPOONS DRIED THYME
375-400G FRESH LASAGNE SHEETS, OR SOME PRE-COOKED
    UNFRESH ONES
300 G MOZZARELLA, COARSELY GRATED
100 G RICOTTA
50G FINELY GRATED PARMESAN

SAUCE

30 G BUTTER OR ¼ CUP EXTRA VIRGIN OLIVE OIL
3 CARROTS, PEELED AND DICED FINELY
2 ONIONS, PEELED AND CHOPPED
3 CELERY STICKS, DICED FINELY
1 MILLION GARLIC CLOVES, PEELED
    AND CHOPPED (JK, 6-8 CLOVES WILL DO)
2 BIRD'S EYE CHILLIES, CHOPPED (OPTIONAL)
SPRIG ROSEMARY
1 CUP RED WINE
1 X 400 G TIN BROWN LENTILS, DRAINED
2 X 400 G TINS WHOLE PEELED TOMATOES
2 TABLESPOONS TOMATO PASTE
1 TABLESPOON BROWN SUGAR
2 CUPS VEGETABLE OR CHICKEN STOCK

GEAR YA NEED

BAKING TRAY LINED
WITH BAKING PAPER

21 X 28 CM BAKING DISH

SPINACH RICOTTA LAYERNATOR

500 G RICOTTA (DELI BASKET RICOTTA -
    THE SHIT THAT COMES IN WATER IN A BASKET)
150 ML MILK
150 G FETA
2 BUNCHES (APPROX. 100 G) ENGLISH SPINACH
HANDFUL BASIL LEAVES

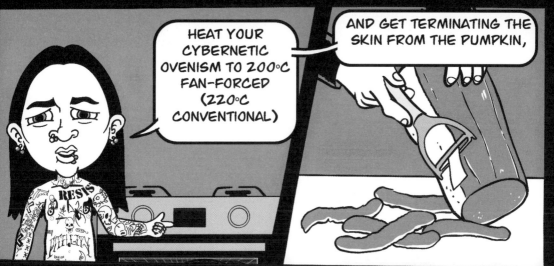

LAY ON A LINED BAKING TRAY

AND DRIZZLE WITH OLIVE OIL,

SCATTER WITH SALT, PEPPER, A PINCH OF CHILLI FLAKES

AND 1 TEASPOON DRIED THYME,

THEN BASH INTO THE OVEN FOR 25-30 MINUTES OR UNTIL TENDER-NATION CAN BE DETECTED.

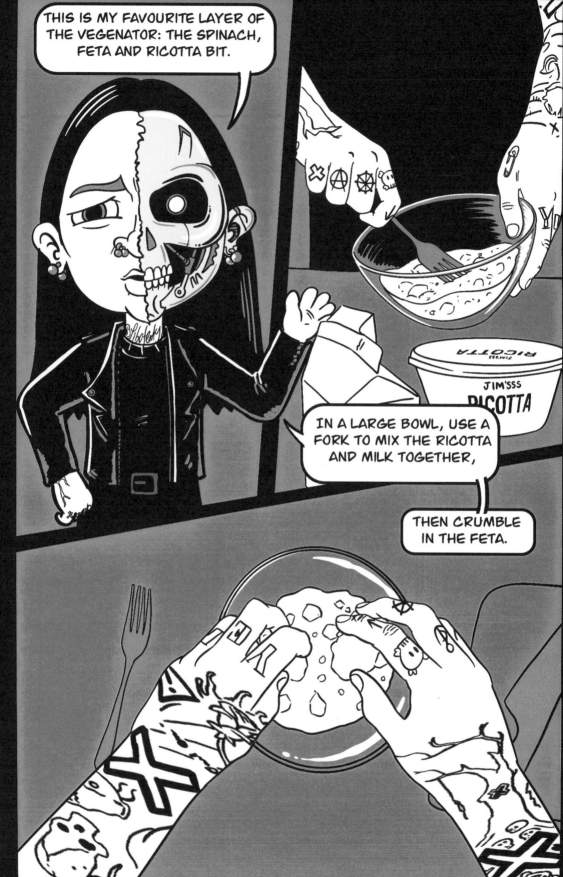

NEXT, COVER WITH A LAYER OF THE PUMPKIN.

BREAK THE SLICES OF PUMPKIN UP TO ACHIEVE GOOD COVERAGE OVER THE PASTA.

NOW GOES IN THAT INCREDIBLE SPINACH,

FOLLOW THIS WITH A THIRD OF THE SAUCE AND A SECOND LAYER OF LASAGNA SHEETS ON TOP OF THAT SHIT.

FETA AND RICOTTA WEAPONRY.

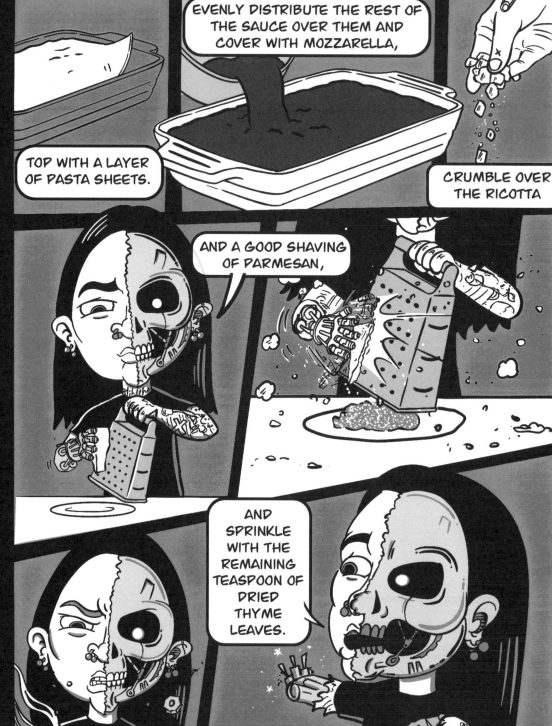

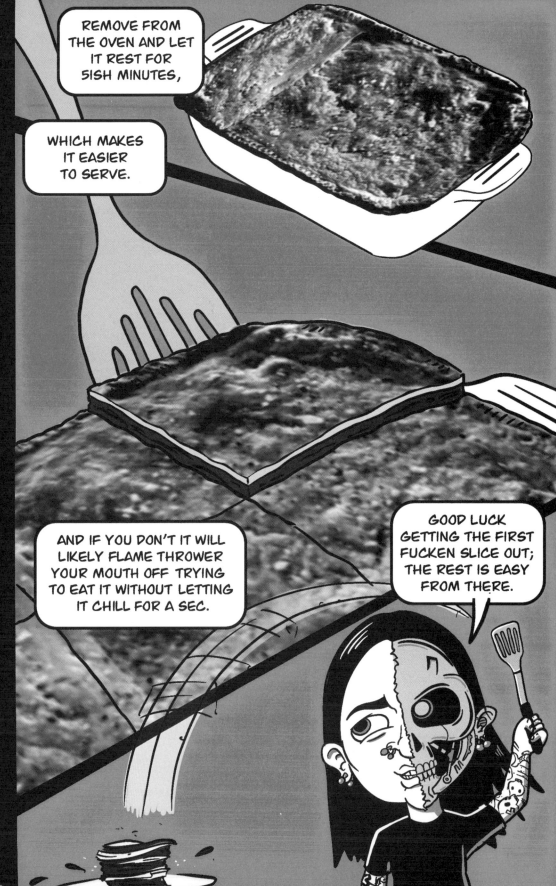

GNOCCH-ON OR FUCK OFF
CHILLI TOMATO GNOCCHI

Harsh name I know, but here's the thing – one of my best mates in the world and I both have matching tattoos on our stomachs that say 'Rock On Or Fuck Off', so I kinda had to. This recipe is an overzealous way of saying go hard or go home, but with gnocchi in mind. You can make gnocchi without potato and just flour that's faster, but we are rockin' the fuck on here, so let's make my favourite type of gnocchi: chilli tomato potato gnocchi.

SERVES:
3–4
COOKING TIME:
a bit over 2 hours

HECTOMETER: 5/10

KEY:
Cheap AF | Comfort Food | Impress the Judges | Vego

INGREDIENTS
GNOCCHI
1 KG SIMILAR SIZED SEBAGO POTATOES (THE DIRTY ONES)
125 G PLAIN FLOUR, PLUS EXTRA TO DUST
1 EGG, LIGHTLY BEATEN
SALT
SHAVED PARMESAN, TO SERVE
SMALL HANDFUL OF BASIL LEAVES, TO SERVE
PEPPER

CHILLI TOMATO SAUCE
1½ TABLESPOONS BUTTER
1 LARGE ONION, PEELED AND DICED
1 FUCKEN WHOLE BULB OF GARLIC (6-8 CLOVES), PEELED AND DICED
3 BIRD'S EYE CHILLIES, DESEEDED AND CHOPPED
2 × 400 G TINS OF CRUSHED OR WHOLE PEELED TOMATOES (SAN MARZANO RULES
IF YOU CAN FIND IT)
1 TABLESPOON BROWN SUGAR
SALT
PEPPER

GEAR:
2 BAKING TRAYS
POTATO RICER (OPTIONAL)

WHEN THAT POINT HAS ARRIVED, REMOVE THEM, LET THEM COOL A LITTLE, 'CAUSE YOU'RE ABOUT TO HANDLE THEM PREFERABLY WITHOUT BURNING THE FUCK OUT OF YOUR HANDS. WHEN THEY'RE COOL ENOUGH, CUT THEM IN HALF AND SCOOP OUT THE FILLING INTO A BOWL AND FUCK THE SKINS OFF TO ANOTHER DIMENSION. NOW MASH THE POTATO, OR EVEN BETTER, 'RICE' IT WITH A POTATO RICER— WHATEVER YOU DO, YOU WANT IT WITH AS FEW LUMPS AS HUMANLY POSSIBLE. MAYBE GET THE FORK OUT AND GET PEDANTIC ABOUT IT. LET THIS EVENT COOL RIIIIIIGHT DOWN IN A BOWL OR ON A TRAY OR ON THE TOP OF EVEREST.

WHILE THAT SHIT IS CHILLING OUT, LET'S MAKE THE SAUCE. INTO A SAUCEPAN OVER A MEDIUM-HIGH HEAT GOES YOUR BUTTER FOLLOWED BY YOUR ONIONS TO COOK OFF FOR 3-4 MINUTES UNTIL SOFTENED, THEN IN GOES YOUR GARLIC AND YOUR CHILLI FOR ANOTHER 1-2 MINUTES. NOW BY ALL MEANS FUCKEN BASH IN A SHITLOAD OF CHILLI IF YOU LOVE IT SICK, LIKE I DO.

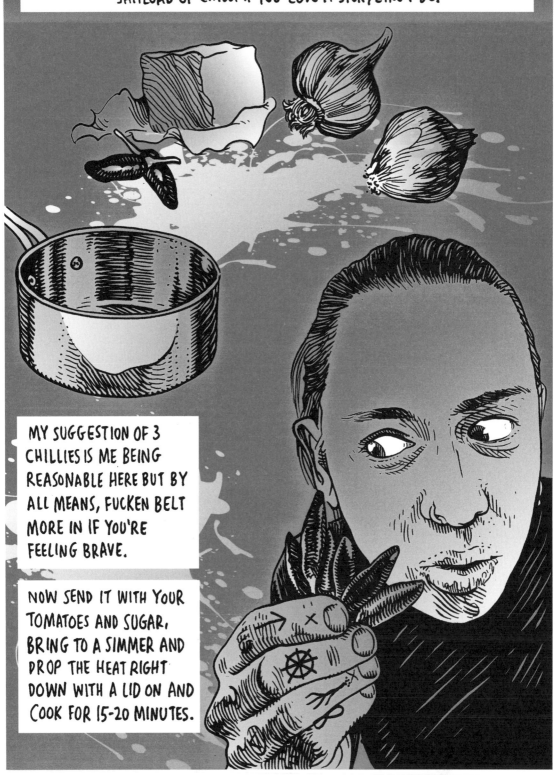

MY SUGGESTION OF 3 CHILLIES IS ME BEING REASONABLE HERE BUT BY ALL MEANS, FUCKEN BELT MORE IN IF YOU'RE FEELING BRAVE.

NOW SEND IT WITH YOUR TOMATOES AND SUGAR, BRING TO A SIMMER AND DROP THE HEAT RIGHT DOWN WITH A LID ON AND COOK FOR 15-20 MINUTES.

WHILE THAT IS CARRYING ON OVER THERE, LET'S MAKE THE GNOCCHI, CHAMPION. GRAB TWO BAKING TRAYS AND COVER EACH WITH BAKING PAPER. THAT COOL, BACKWARDS-HAT-WEARING MASHED POTATO IS GONNA NEED THE FLOUR, EGG AND SALT FOLDED INTO IT. GET IN THERE AND MIX THE FUCKEN SHIT OUT OF IT. IF IT'S STILL WET AND UNMANAGEABLE, ADD MORE FLOUR AS NEEDED OR UNTIL YOU CAN GET IT OUT OF THE BOWL EASILY.

ON A LIGHTLY FLOURED SURFACE DUMP THAT POTATO BALL OUT AND WORK IT LIKE DOUGH, KNEAD IT LIKE YOU MEAN IT FOR AT LEAST 5 MINUTES SO IT'S ALL BLENDED TOGETHER, AGAIN ADDING A LITTLE FLOUR AS YOU GO IF IT'S STICKING TO THE BENCH.

NOW TURN IT ALL INTO A LUMP/BALL AND WITH A LIGHTLY FLOURED KNIFE (YES THERE IS FLOUR ON EVERYTHING BY NOW) CUT THE DOUGH INTO QUARTERS. ROLL ONE SECTION AT A TIME INTO A LONG SAUSAGE-LIKE SHAPE ABOUT 2.5 CM THICK ON A ... WAIT FOR IT ... FLOURED BENCH. RE-FLOUR THAT KNIFE AND CUT THE LOG INTO 3-CM SECTIONS AND PLACE ON THE PREPARED BAKING TRAY.

REPEAT THAT WITH THE REMAINING BALLS OF POTATOEY RADNESS. NOW, YOU CAN FUCK AROUND TRYING TO MAKE EACH GNOCCHI LOOK LIKE THE SHIT YOU SEE IN SOME RESTAURANTS OR IN PACKETS AT THE SHOPS WITH ALL THE COOL FORKED RIDGES IN IT, BUT THE TRUTH IS, THAT SHIT IS A FUCKEN WASTE OF TIME TO ME.

THIS SHAPE YOU END UP WITH LOOKS RAD AND TASTES UNREAL ANYWAY SO DON'T FRET THAT IT DOESN'T LOOK LIKE YOU MIGHT REMEMBER ALL GNOCCHI LOOKING.

BRING A NICE BIG POT OF SALTED WATER TO THE BOIL. WHILE THE WATER IS HEATING UP, GET THE TOMATO SAUCE AND HIT THE FUCKEN THING WITH A STICK BLENDER TO PURÉE IT, ADD SOME SALT AND PEPPER TO TASTE AND SET ASIDE WITH A LID ON IT.

BRZZZRZOOZZ✳!!..✲KRZZRBCH!

You won't believe how quick this next stage is. Once the water is boiling, place in your gnocchi but make sure you don't pack the pot so the gnocchi are as close together as two coats of paint. Just enough at a time so you can see water between the gnocchis. Once they float to the top, they ARE DONE!

Slotted spoon them out into big annoying fancy plates with tiny sunken middles in them, or calm down and use whatever bowls you have at home, and repeat gnocchin' on until they're all cooked.

Chuck the blended sauce over the gnocchi.

Shave over some parmesan, dump on a couple of basil leaves and crack over some pepper.

Fucking gnocch-on or fuck off! That shit rules ...love ya.

SPUD!!

GIMME THE FRITZ

Bloody love a good fritter, but fuck me there are a few trash recipes out there for them. I, too, am responsible for making some rough ones in my time that just fell apart or tasted like poorly thought out ideas. I went on that fucken bananas keto diet once and ate zucchini fritters every day for a month 'cause it was seemingly the only green vegetable I could eat without going over my carb allowance. Spent the whole month hating life and shitting myself. Worst. Anyway, these are bloody awesome and the flour in them means not only are they going to stick together properly, but they're also incidentally going to launch you lovingly out of ketosis in a rocket ship full of flavours.

SERVES:
3–4
COOKING TIME:
around 30 mins

HECTOMETER: 3/10

KEY:
Kiddo Friendly | Quick Sticks | Side Mission | Vego

INGREDIENTZZZ

500 G ZUCCHINI
SALT
225 G PACK HALOUMI
½ CUP SELF-RAISING FLOUR
½ CUP CHOPPED BASIL
I EGG, LIGHTLY BEATEN
PEPPER
½ TEASPOON CHILLI FLAKES,
   OR I FRESH RED CHILLI, DESEEDED
   AND FINELY CHOPPED (OPTIONAL)
EXTRA VIRGIN OLIVE OIL TO SHALLOW FRY
   (5 MM DEEP OF OIL SHOULD GET YOU
   ACROSS THE LINE)
CORIANDER LEAVES, TO SERVE (OPTIONAL)

SALAD

I DESEEDED LEBANESE CUCUMBER
I TOMATO
RED ONION

GARLIC YOGHURT

I CUP GREEK-STYLE YOGHURT
I LEMON, ZESTED
I GARLIC CLOVE, PEELED

AFTER THE BIG 15, DUMP THE MIX IN THE MIDDLE OF A CHUX, A CHEESECLOTH OR A FEW LAYERS OF PAPER TOWEL.

WE WANNA TRY TO SQUEEZE ALL THE WETNESS FROM THE ZUCCHS.

THE PAPER TOWEL IS MORE OF A SQUASHER TO GET IT TO WORK, WHEREAS THE CHUX OR CHEESECLOTH ALLOWS FOR A LITTLE WRINGING ACTION.

REMEMBER THAT EVEN THOUGH CHUX LOOK TOUGH, THEY CAN FUCKEN BUST OPEN IF YOU GIVE IT TOO MUCH THROTTLE.

RETURN THE ZUCCHINI TO THE BOWL.

This is arguably the dish that shot my channel to the next level, but here there's a little twist just to spin you out. How many times have you made a tomato sauce and it just tasted sour or a bit shit? Often a lot of tinned tomatoes are quite fucken tart on their own and need a lot of shit bunged in to get them not to taste like trash. NOT THIS SAUCE, CHAMPION! This sauce is a bloody guaranteed punt straight between the posts. Don't worry, I got you.

SERVES:
6-ish
COOKING TIME:
45 mins–1 hour

HECTOMETER: 2/10

KEY:

Cheap AF | Feed the Team | Low Stress | Quick Sticks | Vego

INGREDIENTS

1 KG RIPE TOMATOES → THE MORE THE MERRIER
1 BROWN ONION
6 CLOVES OF GARLIC, PEELED
2 BIRDS EYE CHILLIES → OPTIONAL
1 TABLESPOON BUTTER
1 TABLESPOON OLIVE OIL
1 CUP RED WINE
HANDFUL FRESH BASIL
2 HEAPED TABLESPOONS TOMATO PASTE
1½ CUPS OF CHICKEN OR VEGGIE STOCK
SALT
PEPPER
½ CUP OF MILK
500G ANY DRIED PASTA
GRANA PADANO OR PARMESAN
  CHEESE TO SERVE

BUY A NICE PASTE
IF YOU CAN, A COUPLE
OF BUCKS EXTRA
GOES A LONG WAY

EQUIPMENT YA GONNA NEED:

STICK BLENDER
SAUCEPAN
  WITH A LID

GRAB YASELF YOUR SAUCEPAN THAT HAS A LID. IF YOU DON'T HAVE A MATCHING LID DON'T SWEAT IT.

I'VE BEEN KNOWN TO USE A STAINLESS STEEL BOWL, ANOTHER PAN OR EVEN A PIZZA TRAY, IT ALL DOES THE SAME FUCKEN JOB.

CHUCK IN YOUR TABLESPOON OF BUTTER AND THE OLIVE OIL AND PLACE OVER A MEDIUM HEAT.

ONCE THE BUTTER IS MELTED CHUCK IN YOUR BOWL OF ONION, GARLIC AND CHILLI (IF USING!).

FRY THAT OFF FOR A FEW MINUTES OR UNTIL THE ONIONS START TO BECOME SLIGHTLY TRANSPARENT.

IF YOU'VE CUT YOUR GARLIC TOO FINELY IT WILL BURN QUICKLY WHICH WE DON'T WANT.

BURNT GARLIC TASTES LIKE SHIT.

IF YOU'RE SERVING THE QUARANTINE SAUCE OVER PASTA, FILL A LARGE SAUCEPAN WITH WATER QUITE BLOODY DEEP.
THE REASON FOR THIS IS THAT WHEN YOU PUT THE PASTA IN THE WATER IT DOESN'T DROP THE TEMPERATURE OF THE WATER SO FAR YOU HAVE TO BRING IT ALL THE WAY BACK TO THE FUCKEN BOIL.
ADD A BIG PINCH OF SALT, PLACE ON THE STOVE AND WHACK A LID ON THAT AND BRING TO THE BOIL.

ONCE THE TOMATOES HAVE GONE SUPER SOFT AND ARE FALLING APART TAKE THE LID OFF AND HIT THEM WITH THE STICK BLENDER.

BLEND IT AS MUCH OR AS LITTLE AS YOU LIKE. PERSONALLY I LIKE IT KIND OF HALFWAY TO TOTALLY PUREED.

NOW FOR THE BIT THAT I'M SURE PEOPLE WILL THINK IS WEIRD BUT IT SLAYS.

ADD THE MILK AND STIR IT IN!

ROAST VEGGIES LIKE A BLOODY CHAMPION!

Roasting is my first love of cooking and one of the great get-together meals. Roast Veggies is not only a fucken powerhouse of the dinner scene but also one of the best ways to eat vegetables, hands down.

There's lots of arguments about how to roast veggies, including whether to parboil or not – really, it's up to you. This is how I like to do it and how to deal with various combinations so everything comes out the oven a big winner. Different veggies have slightly different densities and come in various sizes etc. so it pays to know what to do so you don't make perfect potatoes but carbonise your onions. I'll go through how to deal with each type and how to combine them.

SERVES:
2–6*

COOKING TIME:
Around 1 hour

* depending on whether you serve it as a whole dinner or as sides

HECTOMETER: 2 /10

KEY:
Cheap AF | Feed the Team | Side Mission | Vego

CLASSIC HITS INGREDIENTS

CAN'T HURT TO GIVE ALL THE VEG A RINSE BEFORE KICK-OFF,
AND TRIM OFF ANY PARTS YOU DON'T WANNA EAT.

FOR GROUP VEGGIE ROASTING, I'LL PUT AN ASTERISK NEXT TO
EACH TO GIVE YOU AN IDEA OF HOW THEY GO COOKING
TOGETHER ON ONE TRAY. IF IT HAS 1, THEY CAN BE COOKED
TOGETHER EASILY, 2 CAN JOIN THE 1* GANG BUT WILL NEED LESS
TIME, AND 3 MAY NEED A SOLO TRAY.

POTATOES*
CARROTS*
PARSNIPS*
BEETROOTS*
PUMPKIN**
SWEET POTATOES**
ONIONS**
GARLIC**
BRUSSELS SPROUTS***
ASPARAGUS***

OLIVE OIL
SALT AND PEPPER
HERBS AND SPICES

GEAR

BAKING TRAYS: ANY METAL ONES SHOULD DO: NON-STICK IS NICE
BUT NOT ALWAYS NECESSARY. WORTH NOTING THAT CAST IRON TAKES
A HOT SEC TO WARM UP AND THEN STAYS HOT AF AFTERWARDS, SO
KEEP THAT IN MIND. YOU CAN LINE THEM WITH BAKING PAPER IF THEY
AREN'T NON-STICK, BUT A GOOD BELT OF OIL AND THE OCCASIONAL
SHAKE OF THE TRAY USUALLY DOES THE TRICK.

PRO TIPS

APART FROM BRUSSELS SPROUTS, ALL OF THE FOLLOWING TYPES OF VEG ROAST AT 200°C FAN FAN-FORCED (220°C CONVENTIONAL). HOWEVER, YOUR OVEN MAY BE A BIG LIAR, SO KEEP AN EYE ON HOW THINGS ARE COOKING TO SEE WHEN EVERYTHING LOOKS DONE.

GENTLY PARBOILING YOUR VEG IN SALTY WATER BEFORE ROASTING NOT ONLY HELPS MAKE SURE THAT YOU GET THAT BEAUTIFUL CRISP CRUST ON THE OUTSIDE, BUT ALSO HELPS THE INSIDES TO COOK FULLY.

SO EACH PIECE GETS AN EQUAL COVERING OF OIL AND SEASONING, I PUT THE CUT-UP VEG IN A BOWL AND THEN ADD OIL AND SEASONING (SALT AND PEPPER, FRESH OR DRIED HERBS, SPICES, HONEY ETC) AND GIVE IT ALL A GOOD SWIRL AROUND BEFORE TIPPING IT ONTO THE BAKING TRAY.

SPORTS BALL

WHEN TOO MANY INGREDIENTS OVERCROWD THE TRAY, HEAT FROM IT GETS TRAPPED UNDER THE FOOD AND CREATES STEAM AND SOGGY FOOD WON'T CRISP UP. LEAVING SPACE BETWEEN WHATEVER'S ON YOUR TRAY WILL ALLOW FOR THE BROWNING THAT GIVES SUCH A RAD FLAVOUR.

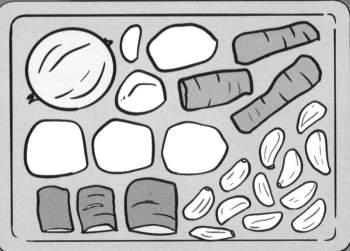

POTATOES

ARGUABLY THE BIG FAVE OF THE ROAST GAME, SPUDS HAVE THAT REPUTATION 'CAUSE THEY ARE FUCKEN GREAT WHEN DONE RIGHT.

NOT ALL POTATOES ARE THE SAME, BUT MOST WILL ROAST OKAY, SOME BETTER THAN OTHERS. I LIKE TO KEEP THINGS FAIRLY STRAIGHTFORWARD WHEN EXPLAINING COOKING SO INSTEAD OF GOING TOO HEAVILY INTO THE THOUSANDS OF FUCKEN POTATO VARIETIES THERE ARE, I'LL JUST SUGGEST A FEW EASY-TO-FIND WINNERS. MY GO-TO FAVES ARE:

DESIREE (OR PRETTY MUCH ANY RED POTATO)

NO BULLSHIT, ALWAYS THE EFFORTLESSLY-PERFECT-FOR-ROASTING POTATO. HAS NEVER GIVEN ME A BUM STEER AND ALWAYS ENDS UP A ROAST DINNER WINNER. GREAT ROASTED 'JACKET' STYLE AKA 'SKIN ON'.

DUTCH CREAM

SLIGHTLY FANCIER AND MORE EXY, I OBSESSED OVER THESE FOR YEARS DUE TO THEIR SUPREME ROASTED TURN-OUT. THEY HAVE A BEAUTIFUL YELLOW, VELVETY CENTRE WHEN DONE RIGHT. NOT SO GREAT FOR MASHING 'CAUSE THEY'RE DENSE ENOUGH TO BE USED AS A SUPPORTING BEAM.

KIPFLER

SIMILAR VIBES TO THE DUTCHIES BUT A SMALLER, LONGER TWISTY-SHAPE THAT YOU WILL USUALLY SPOT STILL COVERED WITH DIRT AND SHIT. WELL WORTH THE DIRT-WASHING JOB THOUGH 'CAUSE THEY ARE FUCKEN AMAZING.

KING EDWARD (WHITE POTATOES)

THE MULTITOOL OF POTATOES, KING TEDS ARE THE MOST WELL-KNOWN, NO FUSS 'ALL-ROUNDERS' GREAT FOR MASH, ROASTING AND THROWING. ALSO GREAT ROASTED IN THE 'JACKET'.

OVEN ALL-STARS

SEBAGO

OVEN ALL-STARS

KING EDWARD

SEBAGO

CHEAP AS A KICK IN THE ARSE AND FUCKEN EVERYWHERE. OFTEN SPOTTED AS BIG DIRT-COVERED UNITS. AGAIN, THEY'RE FLEXIBLE AND GREAT FOR MOST STYLES OF POTATO DISH – ROAST, SOUPS, MASH, DAUPHINOISE, ETC. THEY ROAST WELL BUT ARE A LOT LARGER, SO WILL NEED WASHING AND CUTTING TO SIZE IF BEING ROASTED WITH OTHER VEG.

NEW YORK POTATOE SWISHERS

POTATOES METHOD

THERE IS A RECIPE IN THIS BOOK FOR MY GET FUCKED ROAST POTATOES THAT'S AN AWESOME WAY TO COOK POTATOES, PARTICULARLY ON THEIR OWN OR AS A HERO ADDITION TO ROAST DINNER. IT IS BUT ONE OF MANY WAYS TO ROAST POTATOES (IT WORKS FOR ALL VARIETIES) AND BASICALLY GOES LIKE THIS:

PARBOIL FOR 10-20 MINUTES

ROAST FOR 20-30 MINUTES.

10-20 MINS

20-30 MINS

1) PARBOIL

PARBOILING WORKS FOR ALL POTATOES BUT IS A STERLING ASSIST WITH THE DENSER VARIETIES LIKE DUTCH CREAM OR KIPFLER. YOU CAN LEAVE THE SKINS ON OR OFF. I USUALLY PARBOIL FOR 10-14 MINS, DEPENDING ON THEIR SIZE AND VARIETY – YOU WANT TO AVOID THEM ALL BLOODY FALLING APART: SMALLER/LESS DENSE = FASTER COOKING; BIGGER/DENSER = SLOWER COOKING. IF YOU HAVE DECIDED NOT TO PARBOIL, THEN CUT THEM INTO SMALLER PIECES.

IF YOU KEEP THE SKIN ON, PARBOILING CAN START TO LIFT THE SKIN OFF A LITTLE, PARTICULARLY IF YOU COOK THEM IN THE BOILING WATER FOR LONGER . . . BUT THAT'S OKAY! THE LIFTED SKIN WILL CRISP UP IN THE OVEN AND THAT IS SICK NEWS. DEAD SET, NO ONE ON EARTH WHO LIKES ROAST POTATOES IS GONNA HAVE A FAT OLD SAD ABOUT THAT HAPPENING.

TYPICALLY, A GOOD WAY TO CHECK IF THEY ARE PARBOILED ENOUGH IS BY PRICKING THE POTATOES WITH A FORK. IF THE FORK GOES INTO THE POTATO REASONABLY EASILY, IT'S FUCKEN GOOD TO GO, CHAMPION. DRAIN THEM GENTLY AND LET THEM STEAM IN THE COLANDER FOR A FEW MINUTES TO ENCOURAGE THE EXCESS WATER TO PISS OFF.

OKLAHOMA CITY SPUDS

AVOID CRASH DUMPING THE FUCKEN WHOLE LOT OF BOILED POTATOES INTO A COLANDER LIKE YOU'RE POURING OUT PASTA, OR THEY MAY FALL TO BITS. EASY DOES IT, MUSCLES. WITH THAT SAID, IF THEY GET A LITTLE ROUGHED UP IN THE COLANDER, THAT'S ACTUALLY NOT A BAD SHOUT BECAUSE THE ROUGH EDGES OF THE POTATO WILL SOAK UP THE HERBS, SPICES AND OILS YOU ROAST THEM WITH REALLY WELL AND MAKE A NICE CRUNCH.

2) ROAST

AFTER YOUR PARBOIL, TOSS THE POTATOES GENTLY IN A LITTLE OLIVE OIL ON A BAKING TRAY OR A PREP BOWL WITH A GENEROUS DOSE OF SALT AND A CRACK OF PEPPER IF YOU WISH, THEN HIT IT UP WITH YOUR FAVE FRESH OR DRIED HERBS. TAKE IT SLIGHTLY EASIER AMOUNT-WISE WITH DRIED HERBS - I SEE YOU AND YOUR FISTFUL OF 'MIXED ITALIAN'. DON'T DROWN THEM IN THE STUFF OR YOU'LL BLOW EVERYONE'S HEAD OFF THEIR SHOULDERS WITH TOO MUCH FLAVOUR.

COOK FOR 20 - 30 MINUTES IN THE HOT OVEN, GIVING THE TRAY A SHAKE EVERY NOW AND THEN TO STOP THEM STICKING. HALF-WAY THROUGH, FLIP THEM OVER.

IF YOU WANT THEM TO CRISP UP A LITTLE MORE, CRANK THE HEAT UP AS YOU GO. IF YOU DO, CHECK THEM EVERY 5 MINUTES AS THEY WILL COOK QUICKER.

CARROTS AND PARSNIPS

THERE ARE A COUPLE OF TYPES OF CARROT TO CONSIDER. THE MOST WELL KNOWN IS THE CLASSIC HITS '1 KG BAG' VARIETY. THERE'S ALSO 'JUICING' CARROTS, WHICH JUST MEANS THEY'RE ON THE GEAR (NOT RLY). LOOK, I'M PRETTY SURE THEY ARE JUST THE SAME AS THE OTHER NORMAL SIZED ONES BUT HAPPEN TO BE CHEAPER AND COME IN 5 KG BAGS.

THEN THERE IS MY FAVE, WHICH IS THE BUGS BUNNY-LOOKING DUTCH CARROTS WITH THEIR SILLY GREEN TAILS STILL ATTACHED. THEY ARE SWEET AND FUCKEN BEAUTIFUL FOR ROASTING. AND OF COURSE, LET'S NOT FORGET THE WONDERFUL DYNAMIC WORLD OF PURPLE, YELLOW AND WHITE CARROTS. THESE ARE ALL FUCKEN MAD FOR ROASTING, TOO.

PARSNIPS ARE VERY MUCH IN THE SAME BOAT AS CARROTS AND SHOULD BE COOKED IN THE SAME MANNER.

CARROTS AND PARSNIPS METHOD

 PARBOIL FOR 10 - 15 MINS

THEN ROAST FOR 20 - 30 MINS

CARROT

REGULAR CARROTS

STANDARD 1 KG BAG CARROTS AND PARSNIPS SHARE A POTATO-LIKE DENSITY AND COOK AT A SIMILAR PACE, SO LIKE SPUDS, CHECK THEM WITH A FORK TO SEE IF THEY ARE GOOD TO GO.

DUTCH CARROTS

THESE TEND TO BE SMALLER THAN REGULAR CARROTS, SO PARBOILING ISN'T REALLY NECESSARY IN MY EXPERIENCE. JUST CUT THE GREEN SHIT OFF AND ROAST IN OLIVE OIL, SALT AND ANY FRESH OR DRIED HERBS.

I DON'T PEEL CARROTS OR PARSNIPS BECAUSE FIBRE IS FUCKEN RAD AND GOOD FOR YOUR GUTS AND THEREFORE YOUR ARSE. PEEL OR DON'T PEEL. IT DOESN'T PARRAMATTA, CHAMPION.

PUMPKIN

I USED TO FUCKEN HATE PUMPKIN, I ALSO USED TO LISTEN TO RAP METAL . . . THINGS CHANGE. IT'S ANOTHER STARCHY WINNER WITH LOADS OF BENEFITS: LOW CALORIE, HIGH FIBRE, ORANGE, DELICIOUS.

HOT TIP: WHEN PICKING OUT A PRE-CUT PUMPKIN, LOOK FOR THE RICH ORANGE COLOUR.

THERE ARE SEVERAL TYPES OF PUMPKIN OUT THERE. MY TWO FAVES FOR ROASTING ARE:

KENT

CHEAP, FULL OF FLAVOUR AND A RIPPER TO ROAST, NOT TO MENTION EASY AS ALL GET-OUT TO FIND.

BUTTERNUT

PROBABLY THE SAFEST BET FOR A HESITANT PUMPKIN EATER AND THE ONE THAT HELPED ME GET OVER MY UNREASONABLE DISLIKE FOR PUMPKINS OVERALL. THEY ARE AMAZINGLY SWEET YET MILD, AND THE SKINS ROAST WELL IF YOU DECIDE TO LEAVE THEM ON. GREAT FOR PUMPKIN SOUP, TOO.

PUMPKIN METHOD

AS ALWAYS, THE SIZE OF THE PIECES YOU'RE ROASTING AND THE SPECIFIC TYPE WILL INFLUENCE COOKING TIME. NO NEED TO PARBOIL PUMPKIN. SIMILAR TO DUTCH CARROTS, THEY COOK IN ABOUT 70 PER CENT OF THE TIME AS A POTATO OF THE SAME SIZE.

I LIKE TO SLICE THEM INTO LARGE WEDGES AND JUST HIT THEM WITH OLIVE OIL, SALT AND A HANDFUL OF FRESH ROSEMARY LEAVES.

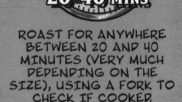

20-40 MINS

ROAST FOR ANYWHERE BETWEEN 20 AND 40 MINUTES (VERY MUCH DEPENDING ON THE SIZE), USING A FORK TO CHECK IF COOKED.

CHARLOTTE SWEET TATERS

SWEET POTATOES

SWEET POTATOES ARE KILLER TO ROAST AND NO PARBOILING IS NECESSARY! TIMING-WISE IN THE ROASTING GAME, THEY ARE SOMEWHERE BETWEEN THE PUMPKIN AND STANDARD POTATO. ALL VARIETIES ARE BADASS. MY FAVE IS THE CLASSIC GOLD SWEET POTATO THAT'S SO COMMON IN AUSTRALIA, BUT THE PURPLE ONES ARE FUCKEN RIGHTEOUS AS WELL.

OVEN ALL-STARS

SWEET 1

SWEET POTATO

SWEET POTATOES METHOD

SKIN ON IS GREAT, SKIN OFF IS ALSO RAD. DRIZZLE OVER OLIVE OIL, A PINCH OF SALT, AND FRESH OR DRIED THYME OR ROSEMARY, EVEN A BIT OF PAPRIKA OR CUMIN GO WELL WITH THEM, TOO. SIZE WILL VERY MUCH DETERMINE THE COOKING TIME GREATLY - ROAST FOR 20-40 MINUTES. WHEN IN DOUBT, THE OLD CHECK WITH A FORK IS THE BEST WAY TO KNOW.

BEETROOT

IF YOU HAVEN'T TRIED A ROASTED BEETROOT THEN YOU'RE FUCKEN MISSING OUT, MATE! EASY AS TO ROAST AND SWEET AS CAN BE, YOU DON'T NEED TO DO MUCH TO THEM SEASONING-WISE IN ORDER TO ADD A FUCKEN PHWOAR FACTOR TO ANY ROAST DINNER. THEY DO HAVE A HABIT OF FUCKEN STAINING THE SHIT OUT OF EVERYTHING THEY TOUCH, SO LOOK OUT FOR THAT IN ALL REGARDS.

ANXIETY WARNING WHEN GOING TO THE BATHROOM AFTER EATING BEETROOT, KEEP IN MIND YOU ATE SOMETHING THAT WAS BEETROOT-COLOURED LAST NIGHT, SO THAT COLOUR YOU'RE SEEING IS THE BEETROOT'S FAULT, IF YA CATCH MY DRIFT?

BEETROOT METHOD

BEETROOT IS AS DENSE AS THEY COME SO IT NEEDS A SOLID PARBOIL BEFORE HITTING THE OVEN. CUT THE STALKS, LEAVES AND HAIRY ARSE OFF IT, PLONK IT IN A POT OF COLD WATER AND BRING TO THE BOIL. IF THEY ARE ABOUT THE SIZE OF A TENNIS BALL THEY WILL GENERALLY NEED TO BE PARBOILED FOR BETWEEN 45 MINUTES AND 1 HOUR BEFORE ROASTING. IF LARGER, THEN LONGER. GIVE IT THE FORK TEST JUST AS YOU DO FOR OTHER VEG. REMOVE FROM THE WATER AND ALLOW TO COOL A LITTLE, THEN YOU CAN REMOVE THE OUTER LAYER OF SKIN IF YOU LIKE. IT SLIPS OFF PRETTY EASILY BUT THEN THINGS CAN GET A BIT STAINY PANTS, SO LEAVE THAT FLOWING WHITE LINEN SUIT YOU BOUGHT AT CLUB MED IN THE WARDROBE, OR JUST USE PAPER TOWEL. DRIZZLE WITH OLIVE OIL, A SPRINKLE OF SALT AND A GRIND OF PEPPER, THEN ROAST FOR 20-40 MINUTES.

20-40 MINS

BRUSSELS SPROUTS

BRUSSELS SPROUTS

. . . ARE THE BUTT OF MANY AN OLD JOKE AND NOT A COMMONLY REQUESTED ITEM, LIKELY DUE TO THEM BEING COOKED TO ABSOLUTE SHIT IN YOUR PAST. BUT TRUST ME WHEN I SAY THAT WHEN ROASTED THEY ACTUALLY GO OFF PARTICULARLY WITH A BIT OF BUTTER AND SALT OR BALSAMIC VINEGAR.

BOSTON BRUSSEL SPROUTS

BRUSSELS SPROUTS METHOD

THEY SHOULD BE COOKED A TOUCH HOTTER THAN THE REST OF YOUR VEGGIES, AND DUE TO THAT MAY NEED THEIR OWN BAKING TRAY OR TO SIT ALONGSIDE THE DENSER VEG LIKE CARROT. JUST TRIM THEIR BASES, CUT 'EM IN HALF, FUCKEN BANG 'EM ON A TRAY, GIVE 'EM A BELT WITH SOME OLIVE OIL AND A LITTLE SALT, EVEN SOME CHILLI FLAKES IF YA FEELING TOUGH, AND WAIT TILL THEY'RE COOKED. 210 - 220°C FAN-FORCED (230 - 240°C CONVENTIONAL) FOR 15 - 30 MINUTES SHOULD DO IT. CHECK WITH A FORK AS USUAL. FINISH WITH A SPRINKLING OF PARMESAN AND A DRIZZLE OF OLIVE OIL.

MILWAUKEE ASPARBUCKETS

ASPARAGUS

YEAH THAT'S RIGHT! I SAID ASPARAGUS AND I MEANT IT! BABY ASPARAGUS COOK FAST SO MAYBE GO FOR THE LARGER/CLASSIC SIZE VARIETY, AND DON'T BOTHER WITH PARBOILING.

ASPARAGUS METHOD

CUT 1 CM OFF THE THICK END, THEN DRIZZLE OVER SOME OLIVE OIL AND SPRINKLE WITH A PINCH OF SALT. SOME CHILLI FLAKES ARE A NICE TOUCH. THROW THEM IN TOWARDS THE END OF YOUR ROAST 'CAUSE THEY COOK FUCKEN QUICK, FOR 5-15 MINUTES, GIVING THE TRAY A QUICK SHAKE HALF WAY. IT'S FAIRLY CLEAR WHEN THEY ARE DONE: THEY LOOK VERY SLIGHTLY BROWNED. AS A SURE SHOT JUST PULL ONE OUT AND TRY IT. IF IT HAS A NICE BITE TO IT, THEN FUCKEN OATH. EVEN IF YOU OVER ROAST THEM THEY STILL TASTE UNREAL WITH SALT AND PEPPER. SOME SHAVED PARMESAN GOES PRETTY HARD, TOO.

OVEN ALL-STARS

ASPARAGUS

ONIONS AND GARLIC

I'VE NEVER HEARD OF SOMEONE BOILING AN ONION OR GARLIC BULB BEFORE THEY ROAST IT, BUT LIFE IS FULL OF SURPRISES SO I'M OPEN TO BEING WRONG ABOUT NOT NEEDING TO. ROASTED BROWN AND RED ONIONS ALONG WITH GARLIC ARE A VERY NICE TOUCH TO ANY ROAST DINNER. JULES GETS VERY SAD IF ROASTED ONION DOESN'T MAKE AN APPEARANCE AT OUR SUNDAY ROAST. SEEING JULES SAD ABOUT FOOD IS TRULY HEARTBREAKING AND I WILL DO ALL I CAN TO PREVENT THAT FROM HAPPENING, SO IT'S A MUST IN OUR HOUSE.

ONIONS AND GARLIC METHOD

I TEND TO ONLY ROAST ONIONS WHOLE IF THEY'RE REAL SMALL ONES, OTHERWISE FOR A MEDIUM OR LARGE ONE I'LL CUT IT INTO HALVES OR QUARTERS THEN DRIZZLE WITH OLIVE OIL. COOKING TIME DEPENDS ON SIZE AND QUANTITY ON THE TRAY, USUALLY BETWEEN 25 AND 40 MINUTES. TOP TIP: IF YOU DON'T CUT THE BOTTOM OFF THE ONION IT WILL STAY TOGETHER BETTER WHEN YOU SERVE IT UP MAYBE JUST DON'T EAT THE COOKED ARSE OF IT.

25-40 MINS

THE GARLIC CAN BE DEALT WITH IN A COUPLE OF WAYS, BOTH METHODS WITH THE SKIN ON. IF ROASTING A WHOLE BULB, JUST REMOVE THE EXCESS FROM THE OUTSIDE OF THE BULB WITHOUT EXPOSING THE ACTUAL CLOVES.

GOLDEN STATE GARLIC

1. PLACE BULB ON THE TRAY, DRIZZLE WITH OLIVE OIL AND DO OTHER SHIT WITH YOUR LIFE.

2. ROAST THE CLOVES INDIVIDUALLY. THE ADVANTAGE IS THEY COOK REAL FAST; THE DISADVANTAGE IS THAT TOO! GREAT IF THE TRAY IS SLAMMED WITH HEAPS OF VEGGIES, AND IF YOU HAVE THE SPACE I PREFER OPTION TWO TO SAVE TIME.

GET FUCKED ROAST POTATOES

Now, I know what you're thinking. 'Are you telling me to get fucked and then just saying roast potatoes?' No, I'm not; I'm merely suggesting that this way of cooking potatoes is so good you'll say 'get fucked' after eating them, or just want to tell everyone to 'get fucked' so you can have them all to yourself. A good roast potato is such an amazing thing, and there are a few cheeky little tricks that will make a huge difference to your taters.

SERVES:
4–6 as a side
COOKING TIME:
around 1.5 hours

HECTOMETER: 2/10

KEY:
Feed the Team | Kid Friendly | Side Mission | Vego

Ingredients

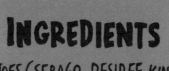

1.5 KG POTATOES (SEBAGO, DESIREE, KING EDWARD)

SALT

150 ML EXTRA-VIRGIN OLIVE OIL

2 TABLESPOONS PLAIN FLOUR

BIG SPRIG OF PURLOINED ROSEMARY, LEAVES
PICKED AND CHOPPED

GARLIC POWDER

SEA SALT FLAKES

PEPPER

BUTTER, TO SERVE (OPTIONAL)

THERE ISN'T A GREAT DEAL TO DO HERE, BUT I ALSO IMAGINE THIS ISN'T THE ONLY FUCKEN THING YOU'RE HAVING TO EAT... ALTHOUGH WITH A NAME LIKE GET FUCKED ROAST POTATOES, YOU MAY BE THAT STOKED WITH THIS DISH THAT YOU WON'T WANNA EAT THE REST OF THE FOOD ONYA PLATE? LET'S SEE HOW WE GO.

COCK THE OVEN HAMMER TO 190°C FAN-FORCED (210°C CONVENTIONAL). IT'S TIME FOR ACTION.

NOW, I'M NOT GOING TO TRY AND EXPLAIN HOW TO PEEL A FUCKEN POTATO, 'CAUSE THAT WOULD SERIOUSLY BE THE MOST BORING SHIT EVER, SO I'LL JUST SUGGEST YOU DO IT. CUT THEM LENGTHWAYS THEN PLACE LOVINGLY INTO A SAUCEPAN AND COVER WITH SALTED COLD WATER. I'VE SAID THIS ON THE CHANNEL A FEW TIMES - WHEN I SAY COLD WATER I DON'T MEAN HOT WATER. **COLD.**

THE REASON IS 'CAUSE THE POTATOES COOK MORE EVENLY THIS WAY, AND WE LIKE TO KEEP THINGS EVEN, STEPHEN.

I KNEW THAT!

BRING THE COLD WATER TO A VERY UN-COLD BOIL AND COOK THE POTATO FOR ABOUT 10-15 MINUTES DEPENDING ON THE SIZE OF THESE BAD BOIZ. WE WANT THEM TENDER BUT NOT AN OVERCOOKED POT OF MEALY RUBBISH. GENTLY STICK IN A FORK OR THE TIP OF A KNIFE TO READ THE VIBE.

GO WITH YOUR GUTS ON THIS ONE..

IT'S DONE!

DRAIN YOUR POTATOES IN A COLANDER, OR YOUR BARE HANDS IF YOU'RE A FUCKING PSYCHO LOOKING TO MAKE A TRIP TO THE EMERGENCY DEPARTMENT.

IT IS NOW MY DUTY TO COMPLETELY DRAIN YOU.

LET THEM REST AND STEAM OUT FOR A FEW MINUTES. WHILE THEY ARE TAKING IT EASY, POUR A GOOD BELT OF OLIVE OIL INTO THE ROASTING TRAY, AND WHACK IT IN THE OVEN.

IF YOU WENT WITH THE LESS SHIT IDEA OF USING A COLANDER, THEN SHAKE THE COLANDER FULL OF POTATOES ABOUT A LITTLE TO KINDA KNOCK THEM AGAINST EACH OTHER AND ROUGH UP THE EDGES A BIT, BUT DON'T SMASH 'EM TOGETHER LIKE SOME KIND OF STRAIGHT-EDGE MOSH PIT WHERE THEY'RE ALL DESTROYED AND FALL TO BITS.

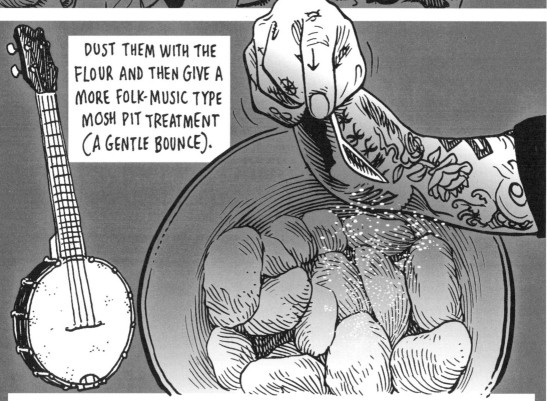

DUST THEM WITH THE FLOUR AND THEN GIVE A MORE FOLK-MUSIC TYPE MOSH PIT TREATMENT (A GENTLE BOUNCE).

PULL THAT HOT AF TRAY OUT OF THE OVEN AND CAREFULLY PLACE THESE POTATOES, CUT SIDE DOWN, INTO THE HOT OIL — VERY CAREFULLY THOUGH, HEY... WE DON'T WANT YOU YELLING 'GET FUCKED' QUITE YET. CHUCK A SMALL HANDFUL OF CHOPPED ROSEMARY OVER THE POTATOES, IF YOU LIKE.

NOW INTO THE OVEN THEY GO THEN. TURN THEM EVERY 20ISH MINUTES UNTIL THE 60-80 MINUTE MARK HAS ARRIVED OR THEY LOOK FUCKEN GOLDEN BROWN.

IF YOU'RE UP FOR IT, A LITTLE SPECIAL SALT GOES HARD WITH THESE, SO I LIKE TO COMBINE A PINCH OF CHOPPED FRESH ROSEMARY WITH HALF A TEASPOON OF POWDERED GARLIC IN A LITTLE DISH WITH SOME SEA SALT FLAKES AND A GRIND OF PEPPER.

PRETTY GET FUCKED GOOD, I TELL YA.

SERVE THEM ON A DISH IN THE MIDDLE OF THE TABLE AND YELL, 'GET FUCKED! HOW GOOD DO THOSE LOOK?' AT EVERYONE. THEN DEVOUR THESE AMAZING POTATOES WITH THAT RAD SALT AND SOME BUTTER, IF YA LIKE.

INCIDENTALLY VEGAN STREET COLESLAW

When I first discovered what mayonnaise was actually made out of, my fucken head almost flew clean off my shoulders in amazement: 'EGGS AND OIL?' I said to my dad. 'Yes,' he replied. There are so many incredible dishes out there that are just as good, if not better, when made as vegan. This here is a champagne example of exactly that; you don't even need the eggs to make a righteous mayo and I'll prove it to ya. The liquid that your canned chickpeas float around in is the replacement for the eggs, and believe it or not it goes off like a vegan frog in a sock.

SERVES:
4–6 as a side
COOKING TIME:
30–45 mins

HECTOMETER: 4/10

KEY:
Impress the Judges | Low Stress | Side Mission | Vegan

INGREDIENTS

- 400 G TIN CHICKPEAS, DRAINED BUT LIQUID RESERVED FOR THE MAYO
- 2 TABLESPOONS EXTRA VIRGIN OLIVE OIL
- SALT
- ½ TEASPOON FINELY GROUND BLACK PEPPER
- 1 TEASPOON CHILLI FLAKES
- ¼ RED CABBAGE
- ¼ WHITE CABBAGE
- 1 SMALL RED ONION, PEELED
- 1 LARGE CARROT, PEELED
- 1 TEASPOON CELERY OR SESAME SEEDS, CRUSHED

VEGAN MAYO

- 2 TEASPOONS DIJON MUSTARD
- ⅓ CUP AQUAFABA (THE LIQUID FROM A CHICKPEA CAN)
- 2 TEASPOONS APPLE CIDER VINEGAR
- 300 ML VEGETABLE OIL
- JUICE OF HALF LEMON
- SEA SALT FLAKES

'WHAT THE FLIP - I NEED AN OVEN FOR THIS?' YEAH, KIND OF.

KINDA

SWITCH YOUR OVEN TO 180°C FAN-FORCED (200°C CONVENTIONAL). LINE A PAN OR TRAY WITH BAKING PAPER.

FETCH YOUR CHICKY BOIZ, DRAIN THE LEGENDARY AQUAFABA (THE LIQUID FROM THEM) INTO A BOWL OR A CUP OR YOUR HAT. CHICKPEAS ARE FUCKING RAD SHIT FOR A LOT OF REASONS, BY THE WAY- THEY ARE A MACRONUTRIENT GOAL-KICKING LORD - AND THEY TASTE LEGENDARY, TOO.

RAD

ONCE YOU'VE RESERVED THE LIQUID FROM THEM, GIVE 'EM A RINSE, PAT DRY AND CHUCK IN A MIXING BOWL WITH 2 TABLESPOONS OLIVE OIL ALONG WITH A PINCH OF SALT, A GRIND OF PEPPER AND THE CHILLI FLAKES.

TOSS ALL THAT TOGETHER AND POUR ONTO THE BAKING TRAY THEN FANG IN THE OVEN FOR 15-20 MINUTES UNTIL CRISPY.

REMOVE AND LET THEM COOL RIGHT DOWN.

MAYBE IT WOULD HELP GET THEM TO COOL FASTER BY PLACING THEM DOWN NEXT TO A FRAMED PHOTO OF THEIR LAST DISAPPOINTING SKI TRIP TO THREDBO, WHERE THE SNOW WAS MORE ICE THAN SNOW BUT IT WAS AT LEAST PRETTY COLD.

AFTER THAT UNDERWHELMING MEMORY HAS WASHED OVER THE CHICKPEAS, SHRED YOUR CABBAGES AND ONION AS FINE AS YOU CAN/LIKE INTO A LARGE BOWL.

YOU CAN USE A MANDOLIN IF YOU OWN ONE (NO, NOT THE SMALL GUITAR) OR A SHARP KNIFE TO GET YOU ACROSS THE LINE. GREAT THE CARROT . . .

NOW GRATE THE CARROT INTO THE BOWL, ADD YOUR SEEDS AND GIVE IT A GOOD TOSS TOGETHER.

NOW LET'S MAYO RAGE.

MAYO RAGE

THE FIRST WAY IS WITH A STICK BLENDER BUNGED INTO A JUG/ CONTAINER JUST WIDER THAN THE HEAD OF THE STICK BLENDER ITSELF.

THERE ARE A FEW WAYS YOU CAN MAKE THIS HAPPEN.

OIL

BLENDANATOR

DRIZZLE

DIJON

AQUAFABA

VINEGAR

WHIZZ UP THE MUSTARD, AQUAFABA AND VINEGAR, THEN SLOWLY DRIZZLE IN THE OIL AS YOU CRANK THE BLENDER UP AND DOWN UNTIL IT MAKES THE MIXTURE INTO A CLASSIC MAYO CONSISTENCY. FINALLY, WHIZZ IN THE LEMON JUICE, AND SALT TO TASTE.

THE SECOND WAY, WHICH I PREFER, IS TO USE A WHISK. SO START WITH THE DIJON, AQUAFABA AND VINEGAR IN A BOWL, WHISKING IT TOGETHER TO COMBINE, BEFORE SLOWLY TIPPING IN THE OIL A BIT AT A TIME AND WHISKING THE FUCK OUT OF IT UNTIL IT GETS THICK ENOUGH, FOLLOWED BY THE LEMON AT THE END AND SALT.

WHISK WHISK WHISK

SQUEEZE

MAYO

WHISK

AGAIN, TASTE IT, AND WHEN IT SUITS YOU, YOU'RE READY TO WALK INCIDENTALLY DOWN VEGAN COLESLAW STREET.

ADD ⅔ CUP OF THAT AWESOME 'SLAUWCE' TO YOUR VEG BOWL (THE REST WILL KEEP IN THE FRIDGE FOR A COUPLE OF WEEKS), FANG IN YOUR CRISPY CHICKPEAS ALONG WITH A PINCH OF SALT AND A CRACK OF PEPPS IF YOU WANNA AND TOSS IT ALL TOGETHER.

FEEL FREE TO ADD MORE OF THE MAYO IF YOU LIKE IT A BIT MORE SAUCE HEAVY, IT'S YOUR ADVENTURE, ZELDA.

NOW THAT, MY FRIEND, IS A FUCKEN BEAUTY OF A COLESLAW AND NOT A SICKLY-SWEET BOWL OF WET SHIT THAT BELONGS IN THE CONFECTIONARY SECTION.

SERVE POSSIBLY WITH THE VERY UN-VEGAN CHICKEN WINGS WE HAVE A RECIPE FOR IN THIS VERY BOOK OR WITH WHATEVER AND WHOEVER YOU LIKE.

(NOT EVEN SHIT) RAD SALAD

Fucken hell, haven't we all suffered a plethora of heinous salads in our lives that either tasted as if they crawled out of a lawn mower's arse or like someone tipped five tonnes of airline-food-level vinaigrette on a tree. It's fair enough that the word 'salad' often strikes bored fear into the hearts of many. Well I've had a gutful of living life in the grass lane! Let's change the game up and make a salad that doesn't make you want to put your head in your hands and wish you'd made almost anything else on earth.

SERVES:
3–4
COOKING TIME:
less than 30 mins

HECTOMETER: 3/10

KEY:
Cheap AF | Kiddo Friendly | Low Stress | Side Mission | Vego

INGREDIENTS

75 G PINE NUTS
150 G ROCKET LEAVES
2 LEBANESE CUCUMBERS, SLICED THINLY
I PEACH, DESTONED AND CHOPPED
150 G GOAT'S CHEESE, CRUMBLED
I TABLESPOON EXTRA-VIRGIN OLIVE OIL
I AVOCADO, SLICED

DRESSING

PINCH SEA SALT FLAKES
CRACK OF PEPPER
1-2 TABLESPOONS WARM WATER
⅔ TABLESPOON DIJON MUSTARD
I TABLESPOON BALSAMIC VINEGAR
50 ML EXTRA-VIRGIN OLIVE OIL

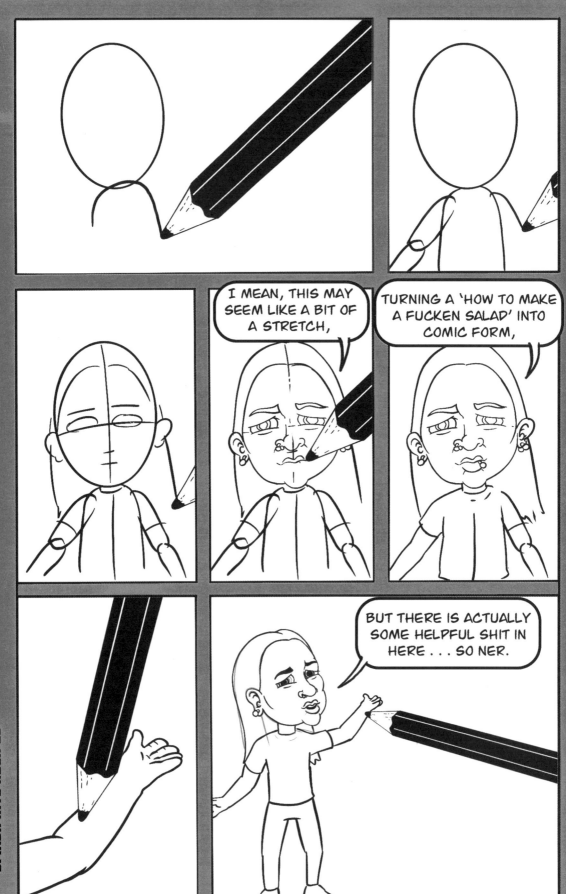

LET'S START WITH THE PINE NUTS. YOU MAY NEED TO REMORTGAGE YOUR HOUSE TO AFFORD THEM, BUT YOU DON'T NEED HEAPS. LET ME EXPLAIN WHAT TOASTING PINE NUTS DOES AND DOESN'T MEAN: IT DOESN'T MEAN DUMP THEM INTO THE FUCKEN TOASTER,

'CAUSE THAT SHIT WON'T WORK (THOUGH IT WILL SMELL NICE TRYING TO COOK THEM LIKE THIS, EVEN IF IT MAY ROYALLY FUCK YOUR TOASTER).

GET YOURSELF A NICE FLAT-BOTTOMED FRYING PAN, AND BUNG IT OVER A MEDIUM-HIGH HEAT.

NOW, DON'T PUT ANY OIL IN THE THING 'CAUSE THIS BIT OF THE RECIPE DOESN'T EVEN NEED IT.

ONCE THE PAN IS WARM, FANG IN THE PINE NUTS AND ROLL THEM AROUND UNTIL THEY JUST START TO TURN A TOUCH BROWN. THEY SHOULD SMELL INSANELY RAD TOO, WHICH IS GREAT 'CAUSE THIS IS A RAD SALAD.

ONCE YOU'VE HIT THAT POINT OF SEMI TOASTEDNESS, TURN THE HEAT OFF, TIP THEM FROM THE PAN INTO A BOWL AND SET ASIDE.

I MEAN, THERE'S NOT A GREAT DEAL HERE THAT YOU NEED TO KNOW OTHER THAN HOW TO MAKE THE DRESSING. THIS SALAD HAS ENOUGH GOING ON THAT YOU SHOULDN'T NEED TO DROWN THE FUCK OUT OF IT WITH 4 LITRES OF DRESSING – IN FACT, THAT APPROACH SHITS ME TO TEARS. IF I WANTED TO GO FOR A SWIM I WOULD BE WEARING MY SPEEDOS RIGHT NOW.

THIS DRESSING IS JUST ENOUGH TO TIP ITS HAT TO THE INGREDIENTS WITHOUT SHAKING YOU BY THE SHOULDERS WITH DEMANDS OF MORE FLAVOUR.

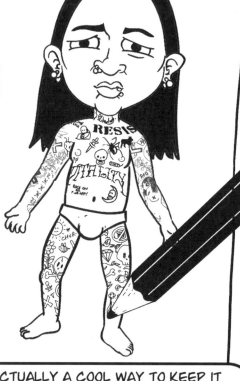

IT'S ACTUALLY A COOL WAY TO KEEP IT LIGHT AND GET ALL THE FLAVOURS TO HANG TOGETHER BEFORE YOU ADD YOUR OIL.

WATER SOUNDS LIKE A WEIRD INGREDIENT,

THIS IS A COOL LITTLE TRICK MY DAD SHOWED ME.

ADD A PINCH OF NICE SALT FLAKES AND A CRACK OF PEPPER TO A GLASS, A JAM JAR OR A SMALL BOWL.

NOW, USE A TABLESPOON OR TWO OF WARM WATER TO DISSOLVE THE SALT AND PEPPER, KICKING IT ABOUT WITH A TEASPOON,

THEN ADD YOUR DIJON AND BALSAMIC VINEGAR.

LEAVE THE OLIVE OIL FOR LAST –

ONLY ONCE EVERYTHING ELSE IS COMBINED DO YOU WANT TO FANG THAT IN AS WELL.

DOESN'T HURT TO HAVE A GOOD QUALITY EXTRA-VIRGIN OLIVE OIL ON HAND, AS OBVIOUSLY THE BETTER THE OLIVE OIL, THE BETTER THE END RESULT WILL TASTE. CHEAPER STUFF CAN TOTALLY TASTE AWESOME TOO, SO DON'T STRESS IF YOU CAN'T AFFORD SUPER FANCY STUFF.

OIL BARON

GO FOCACCIA YOURSELF

Well, didn't everyone flip their fucken lids at making sourdough about three years ago? Not me, mate! I was too busy cooking way easier-to-manage bread nonsense that doesn't need a babysitter to camp out in my fridge and read bread starter bedtime stories.

This is easy and no-nonsense bread that doesn't need you to hold its hand, cater to its every need and feed it full of bullshit just to hang out with it. Instead, drive this super straightforward classic into your repertoire with any variety of herbs, cherry tomatoes, thinly-sliced potatoes, olives and whatever tonne of other bananas shit from the 80s you can think of, and if anyone asks you, 'Why didn't you just make sourdough?' you can tell them 'cause it looks like it's got enough mates and you're too busy focaccia-ing yourself to give a shit. K thx.

SERVES:
6–8
COOKING TIME:
Under an hour
(dough resting time 2–48 hours)

HECTOMETER: 3.5/10

KEY:
Cheap AF | Feed the Team | Kiddo Friendly | Side Mission | Vego

INGREDIENTS

2 CUPS OF WARM WATER (NOT HOT)

7G DRY YEAST

2 TEASPOONS SUGAR

4 CUPS BREAD FLOUR/PLAIN FLOUR

GOOD DOSE OF ROCK SALT

FEW SPRIGS OF ROSEMARY, THYME
OR ANY HERBS YA LIKE

OLIVE OIL

BALSAMIC VINEGAR AND OLIVE OIL,
TO SERVE

GEAR

25 x 25cm OR 30 x 25cm NON-STICK
BAKING TRAY

THIS IS HOW FUCKEN EASY THIS SHIT IS:

MEASURE YOUR WARM WATER INTO A SMALL BOWL AND ADD YOUR DRIED YEAST AND SUGAR,

STIR TOGETHER AND LET IT SIT FOR A SECOND.

NOW,

At this point in my video I added my salt to the water and hundreds of the most upset people ever, not realising they were watching a free video, took their important life-saving time to let me know that I had totally fucked the bread by putting salt with the yeast. To be honest, I don't give a fuck and it turned out great, so suffer in ya jocks, ya keyboard sourdough warriors!

WITH THAT SAID...

...NOW IS THE TIME, INTO ANOTHER SEPARATE AND MUCH LARGER BOWL, TO SIFT YOUR FLOUR.

ADD YA SALT TO THE DRY FLOUR NOW IF YOU WANNA OBEY THE LAW AND AVOID PERSECUTION BY THE BREAD POLICE.

MAKE A WELL IN THE CENTRE OF THE SALTY FLOUR.

ADD THE SWEET YEASTY WATER AND FOLD TOGETHER WITH A SILICON SPATULA.

..wood ones are *dogshit for this.*

IF YOU HAVE ONE OF THOSE FANCY FUCKEN STANDING MIXER THINGS, THEN BY ALL MEANS I'LL JUST SEE MYSELF OUT WHILE YOU USE THAT THEN, YA FANCY PANTS.

DRIZZLE IN A GOOD BELT OF OLIVE OIL —

(2-3 TABLESPOONS)

— AND KEEP ON FOLDING IT TOGETHER.

ONCE COMBINED INTO A TIDY-ISH BALL, DRIZZLE A FINAL GLUG OF OLIVE OIL OVER IT AND COVER IT IN WHATEVER YOU USE TO COVER SHIT AIRTIGHT IN YOUR HOUSE AND BANG IN THE FRIDGE FOR 24 - 48 HOURS —

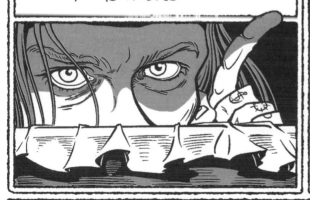

yes, that long. In fact, long enough to watch every episode of Seinfeld back-to-back.

BY THAT POINT YOU WANNA PULL IT OUT OF THE FRIDGE AND GIVE IT ANOTHER TABLESPOON OR SO OF OLIVE OIL. CAREFULLY FOLD EACH SIDE INTO THE CENTRE LIKE YOU'RE STUFFING TISSUE PAPER INTO A... CAMRY'S REAR PARCEL SHELF. MAYBE 5 OR 6 FOLDS MAX AND LEAVE IT.

THE THICKNESS OF YOUR FOCCACIA CAN BE DETERMINED BY THE SIZE AND DEPTH OF YOUR BAKING TRAY. AS LONG AS IT'S AT LEAST 4 OR 5 CENTIMETRES DEEP, IT SHOULD BE SWEET. USE YET MORE OLIVE OIL TO GREASE THE SHIT OUT OF A 25×25cm OR A 30×25cm NON-STICK BAKING TRAY, THEN FOR SOME REASON PLACE BAKING PAPER ON TOP OF THAT PLUS A DRIZZLE OF OLIVE OIL IN THE MIDDLE OF THE PAPER.

This seems non-stick extra af but it's a failsafe that works for me. Feel free to not bother with the baking paper and cross ya fingers that all that non-stick shit is doing its job.

DUMP THE DOUGH DIRECTLY ON TOP OF THE OLIVE OIL AND EVER-SO-GENTLY FROM THE CENTRE OUTWARDS, EVENLY SPREAD THE DOUGH WITH YOUR FINGERS TILL IT REACHES THE EDGE OF THE TRAY OR PRETTY CLOSE.

NOW POKE YOUR FINGERS ALL OVER THE WHOLE FOCACCIA TO GIVE IT A LUMPY LOOK, PRESSING YOUR FINGERS RIGHT DOWN TO THE BOTTOM TILL YOU ALMOST FEEL THE TRAY. IT DOESN'T HAVE TO BREAK THE DOUGH BUT WON'T HEAPS MATTER IF YOU DO.

COVER IN FRESH HERBS LIKE ROSEMARY AND/OR THYME, A GOOD DOSE OF ROCK SALT.

... AND **MORE FUCKEN OLIVE OIL!!**

COVER AND LET SIT FOR AN HOUR OUT OF THE FRIDGE SOMEWHERE WARM.

DIE, SHITTY FROZEN APPLE PIE

Apple pies are great, but not when they are those pre-made loads of shit from the frozen food aisle at the shops. Apple pies are a nostalgic classic that truly deserve more respect than a freezer burnt discus can offer. I will acknowledge the irony in needing to go to the frozen food aisle to buy the pastry, but this does give you a chance to flip off the deadshit frozen apple pies nearby as you walk away feeling very full of yourself . . . and soon to be pie. Kick a goal straight between the posts at the dinner table by adding this fucken beauty to your repertoire – you won't be disappointed.

SERVES:
8–10
COOKING TIME:
1½–2 hours

HECTOMETER: 6/10

KEY:
Cheap AF | Comfort Food | Feed the Team |
Impress the Judges | Vego

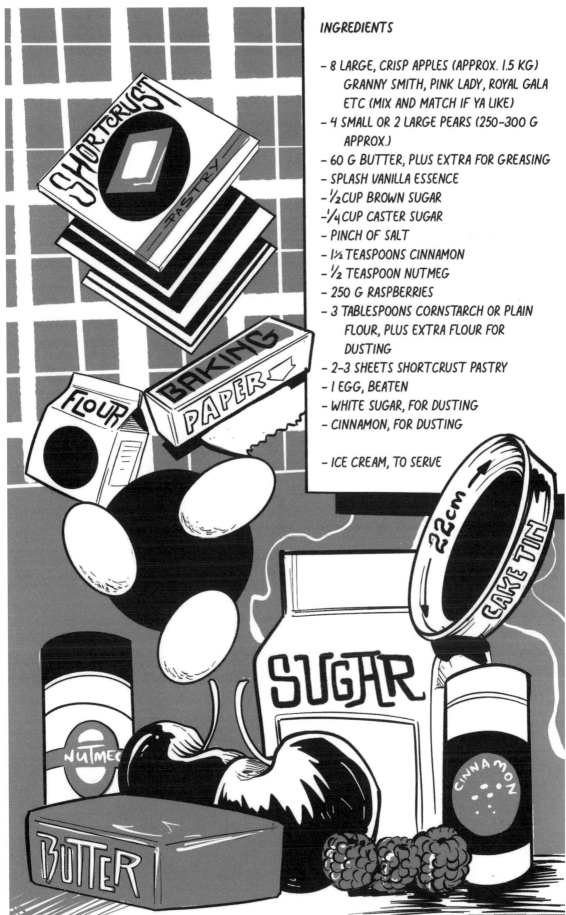

INGREDIENTS

- 8 LARGE, CRISP APPLES (APPROX. 1.5 KG) GRANNY SMITH, PINK LADY, ROYAL GALA ETC (MIX AND MATCH IF YA LIKE)
- 4 SMALL OR 2 LARGE PEARS (250–300 G APPROX.)
- 60 G BUTTER, PLUS EXTRA FOR GREASING
- SPLASH VANILLA ESSENCE
- $\frac{1}{2}$ CUP BROWN SUGAR
- $\frac{1}{4}$ CUP CASTER SUGAR
- PINCH OF SALT
- 1½ TEASPOONS CINNAMON
- $\frac{1}{2}$ TEASPOON NUTMEG
- 250 G RASPBERRIES
- 3 TABLESPOONS CORNSTARCH OR PLAIN FLOUR, PLUS EXTRA FLOUR FOR DUSTING
- 2–3 SHEETS SHORTCRUST PASTRY
- 1 EGG, BEATEN
- WHITE SUGAR, FOR DUSTING
- CINNAMON, FOR DUSTING

- ICE CREAM, TO SERVE

PEEL THE APPLES AND REMOVE THEIR CORES AND SEEDS, 'CAUSE IF YOU EAT THE SEEDS YOU WILL GROW A TREE INSIDE YOU (NOT REALLY; THEY JUST TASTE LIKE SHIT AND WILL CRACK YOUR VENEERS, MICHAEL).

SLICE THEM INTO ½ CM WEDGES AND BUNG IN A BOWL.

IT IS COMMON BEHAVIOUR FOR PEOPLE TO HAVE A FUCKEN MELTDOWN ABOUT THE APPLES TURNING BROWN ONCE THEY'VE BEEN PEELED, SO TO REMEDY THIS HUGE DILEMMA A LOT OF PEOPLE TOSS THEM THROUGH LEMON JUICE TO PREVENT IT.

APPLES!!

AWWW NOOO... MY POOR APPLES

YOU ARE OF COURSE WELCOME TO CARRY ON IN THIS MANNER, BUT SOON YOU WILL COME TO REALISE THAT THEY GO THAT FUCKEN BROWN COLOUR ANYWAY WHEN YOU BLOODY COOK THEM. HEY, IT'S YOUR TIME AND BY ALL MEANS WASTE MORE OF IT DOING POINTLESS SHIT... MAYBE PEEL THE RASPBERRIES WHILE YOU'RE AT IT.

PEEL AND CORE THE PEARS AND GRATE THEM INTO THEIR OWN BOWL.

IN A SMALL SAUCEPAN OVER MEDIUM HEAT, COOK THE GRATED PEARS FOR 5-7 MINUTES TO EVAPORATE SOME OF THEIR LIQUID, THEN IN THE SAME SAUCEPAN OVER THE SAME HEAT, MELT THE BUTTER AND FANG IN YOUR APPLES. STIR AND GENTLY COOK FOR 5-7 MINUTES UNTIL THEY START TO CHANGE COLOUR SLIGHTLY. AT THIS STAGE BUNG IN YOUR VANILLA, SUGARS, A PINCH OF SALT AND SPICES.

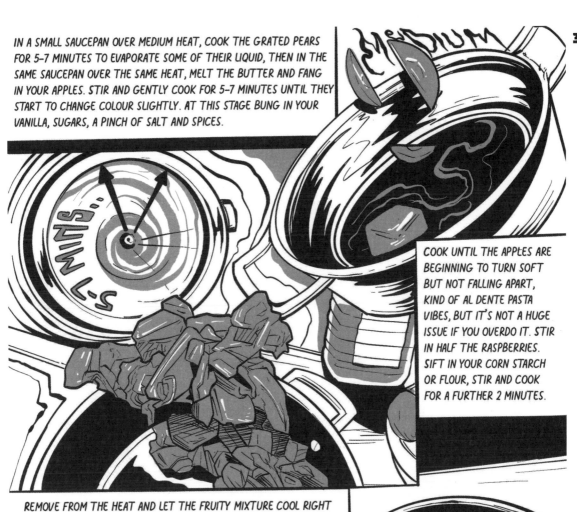

COOK UNTIL THE APPLES ARE BEGINNING TO TURN SOFT BUT NOT FALLING APART, KIND OF AL DENTE PASTA VIBES, BUT IT'S NOT A HUGE ISSUE IF YOU OVERDO IT. STIR IN HALF THE RASPBERRIES. SIFT IN YOUR CORN STARCH OR FLOUR, STIR AND COOK FOR A FURTHER 2 MINUTES.

REMOVE FROM THE HEAT AND LET THE FRUITY MIXTURE COOL RIGHT DOWN.

IF YOU'RE IN A REAL HURRY MAYBE NECK A CAN OF ENERGY DRINK, TURN YOUR HAT BACKWARDS, CRANK SOME RAP METAL AND DO A BUNNY-HOP ON YA SICK HUFFY. THAT SHOULD REALLY SPEED UP THE COOL, DUDE!

NOW LET'S MAKE THE PIE BIT.

GET THE OVEN KICKED OFF TO A SWEET 200°C FAN-FORCED (220°C CONVENTIONAL).

REMOVE THE SHORTCRUST FROM THE FREEZER TO THAW ON THE BENCH.

READY UP YOUR 22 CM PIE TIN BY SITTING IT ON TOP OF A SQUARE OF BAKING PAPER, TIN FACING OPEN SIDE UP.

TO LINE THE BASE OF THE TIN WITHOUT SHOVING HALF A BIBLE'S WORTH OF UNNECESSARY PAPER INTO IT, PLACE IT ON A SHEET OF BAKING PAPER AND RUN THE BLADE OF A KNIFE AROUND THE OUTSIDE OF THE TIN. THIS WILL CREATE A SPECIAL LITTLE CIRCLE ON THE BAKING PAPER THAT WILL MAKE A RIPPER PERFECT-FITTING NON-STICK LINING FOR THE BASE OF THE INSIDE OF YA TIN.

GENEROUSLY GREASE UP THE PAN WITH BUTTER AND PLACE THE LITTLE CIRCLE OF BAKING PAPER INSIDE ON THE BASE.

THE SECOND APPROACH IS TO FRANKENSTEIN A CUPPLA FUCKEN SHEETS TOGETHER SO YOU HAVE A BIGGER BIT OF PASTRY TO LAY OVER THE PAN TO BEGIN WITH.

THIS CAN BE DONE BY PRESSING TWO SHEETS TOGETHER WITH A LITTLE BIT OF WATER BETWEEN THE JOINS, THIS SHOULD EFFECTIVELY GLUE THEM TOGETHER. THE ONLY POSSIBLE ISSUE HERE IS IT CAN BE TRICKY AND POSSIBLY CREATE A HOLE IN THE ARSE OF THE PIE.

EITHER WAY IS FINE THOUGH, AND IF YOU ACCIDENTALLY BUST HOLES IN THE PASTRY, A LITTLE BIT OF PATCH WORK WITH A SMALL DASH OF WATER TO BIND BITS OF PASTRY TO THE HOLES IS ACCEPTABLE BEHAVIOUR IN MY BOOK.

H2O

SPLASH

LAY WHATEVER STYLE OF PASTRY SHEET/S ACTION YOU WENT WITH INTO THE BUTTERED TIN VERY CAREFULLY, ENSURING IT FILLS THE PAN AND LEAVES ENOUGH TO GO OVER THE SIDES A TOUCH. THERE'S A TRICK TO GENTLY ENCOURAGE PASTRY OVER THE BASE AND SIDES WITHOUT BUNGING HOLES IN IT.

THE KEY IS TO NOT HAVE ALL EDGES PRESSED DOWN BEFORE YOU PUSH THE CENTRE TO THE SIDES, SO SLOWLY WORK YOUR WAY FROM THE MIDDLE OUTWARDS, THEN PRESS DOWN AROUND THE EDGE TO FORM A RIM.

FORK MAYBE FIVE OR SIX SMALL FORK HOLES IN THE BASE. THIS STOPS ITS BELLY RISING WHEN WE BLIND BAKE THE BASE.

IT'S A THING TO USE BAKING BEANS OR RICE ATOP BAKING PAPER TO HELP IT SIT WHILE BAKING BUT I DON'T LIKE WASTING THE RICE AND I DON'T OWN BAKING BEANS. BY ALL MEANS USE THAT TECHNIQUE IF YOU'RE INTO IT, THOUGH.

STICK THE BASE IN THE OVEN FOR 10-12 MINUTES UNTIL THE PASTRY HAS COOKED A LITTLE AND THEN REMOVE AND COOL ON THE BENCH.

BAKING BEANS

BAKING BEANS

RICE

FILL WITH THE COOLED FRUIT FILLING, EVENLY SPREAD OVER THE BASE, AND TURN YOUR ATTENTION TO MAKING A LID.

IF YOU HAVE ANY PATIENCE OR MENTAL HEALTH LEFT, YOU'RE WELCOME TO ATTEMPT THE MIGHTY CROSSHATCH OF PASTRY AS THE LID.

ANXIETY

I TRIED THIS SEVERAL TIMES AND MY ANXIETY AND ADHD WENT OFF LIKE A FUCKEN SHIT FIREWORK SHOW. STILL, I WAS PROUD TO GET THERE IN THE END.

ADHD

BREAK DOWN

IT'S OK

IF YOU'RE THE PROUD TYPE YOU CAN DO THIS BY CUTTING THE PASTRY INTO LONG, 1.5 CM WIDE STRIPS AND LAYING THEM IN A CRISS CROSS, OVER-AND-UNDER PATTERN OVER THE FILLING, SECURING THE EDGES DOWN WITH AN ADDITIONAL RING OF PASTRY TO HOLD YOUR PLAITED MASTERPIECE IN PLACE, THEN EGG WASHING IT WITH BEATEN EGG PAINTED ONTO THE PASTRY.

AND THEN, 'CAUSE THAT'S NOT ENOUGH, YOU PUT THE REMAINING RASPBERRIES IN THE GAPS AND DUST THE LOT WITH SUGAR AND CINNAMON.

IT'S VERY CUTE AND THE LID OF THE PIE LOOKS LIKE IT DOES ON A TOM AND JERRY CARTOON, BUT THAT DOESN'T MAKE IT NECESSARILY ANY BETTER.

FASHUN

AS THEY SAY, FASHION IS PAIN.

THE OTHER WAY LESS INTENSE OPTION IS JUST FUCKEN SCATTER THE REMAINING RASPBERRIES OVER THE FILLING AND LAY A FLAT LID OF PASTRY OVER THE TOP, PRESSING THE SIDES AND TRIMMING THE EXCESS PASTRY. THEN ALL THERE IS TO DO IS EGG WASH IT AND LIGHTLY SUGAR AND CINNAMON THE FUCKEN THING. YOU'LL WANT TO PUT A FEW KNIFE HOLES IN THE LID BEFORE YOU COOK IT OR IT WILL FUCKEN BLOW A VALVE.

PUFF PASTRY

YOU CAN ALSO USE PUFF PASTRY FOR THE TOP OF THE PIE IF YOU LIKE A PUFFY TOP, USING THE SAME TECHNIQUE.

TURN THE OVEN DOWN TO 180°C FAN-FORCED (200°C CONVENTIONAL) FROM ITS PREVIOUS HEAT AND BAKE FOR 45-50 MINUTES UNTIL GOLDEN BROWN ON TOP, ROTATING AT THE HALFWAY MARK SO THE PASTRY COLOURS UP EVENLY.

BUT AS ALWAYS, GO WITH YOUR GUT, IF IT LOOKS LIKE IT'S COOKED SOONER OR YOUR OVEN IS A FUCKEN LIAR LIKE MINE THEN GO WITH WHEN YOU RECKON IT'S READY.

Minutes

45-50

180°C
200°C

REMOVE FROM THE OVEN AND LET IT REST FOR A BIT 'TILL IT'S COOLED BEFORE REMOVING FROM THE DISH. THREE HOURS ISN'T UNHEARD OF.

VANILLA

SERVE WITH ICE CREAM OR A LIE DOWN AFTER MAKING THAT FUCKEN RIDICULOUS LID.

ONYA SONYA.

JIM'S TIRAMEEZOO

If you are wondering who the flip Jim is, it's worth a dig through the back catalogue of my channel to find some of the weirdest face-swapping (and at times rubber mask) character videos I've made. I developed him as a representation of the classic old Aussie fella who likes the simple things in life, and at the same time he's a little eccentric and has a habit of getting a little carried away . . . my future, I'm sure. If there is one thing I know about Jim, it's that he loves a coffee or forty, as well as the occasional scoop of Blue Ribbon. He has been known at times to fondly combine those two flavours in a word he pronounces with his oh-so-Australian timbre: 'tirameeezooooo'. As an homage to the great man himself, here is a ripper of a tiramisu that he would be more than happy to put away all by himself.

SERVES:
8
COOKING TIME:
under an hour
(resting time:
a few hours to overnight)

HECTOMETER: 6/10

KEY:
Comfort Food | Feed the Team | Impress the Judges | Vego

INGREDIENTS

6 EGG YOLKS
1 CUP CASTER SUGAR
2 TEASPOONS VANILLA EXTRACT
375 G MASCARPONE, AT ROOM TEMPERATURE
500 ML THICKENED CREAM
1½ CUPS FRESHLY BREWED, STRONG COFFEE
½ CUP MARSALA OR OTHER LIQUEUR (LIKE FRANGELICO)
300 G SAVOIARDI (LADY FINGER) BISCUITS
¼ CUP DARK COCOA POWDER

GEAR:
22 CM SQUARE DISH

GET YOUR WHISKING ARM READY, MUSCLES. IN A HEATPROOF BOWL WHISK TOGETHER THE EGG YOLKS AND ¾ CUP SUGAR TILL COMBINED.

ON THE STOVE YOU'RE GONNA WANNA GET A POT GOING WITH A FEW INCHES OF WATER ON THE BOIL. THIS SAID POT NEEDS TO BE A CONVENIENT SIZE THAT CAN FIT THE PREVIOUSLY MENTIONED BOWL ON TOP OF IT WITHOUT IT FUCKEN FALLING INTO THE POT OR TOUCHING THE WATER.

REST THE MIXING BOWL CAREFULLY ON TOP OF THE POT OF BOILING WATER (AGAIN MAKING SURE THE WATER IS STEAMING THE BOWL RATHER THAN ACTUALLY TOUCHING THE BOWL), AND WHISK AWAY FOR 6-8 MINUTES, UNTIL THE MIXTURE HAS THICKENED UP AND TURNED A PALE COLOUR.

THEN REMOVE IT FROM THE STEAMY POT AND SET ASIDE TO CHILL OUT FOR A WHILE TILL IT COOLS OFF.

ONCE COOL, WHISK IN THE VANILLA AND MASCARPONE (THE ONLY CHEESE USED TO HIDE A HORSE). ALL THAT NONSENSE, INCLUDING THAT SHIT HORSE JOKE, CAN CONTINUE TO RELAX FOR A BIT WHILE YOU GET ON WITH YOUR COMEDY CAREER AND THE REST OF THE DISH.

POUR THE CREAM INTO A LARGE BOWL. NOW COMES THE TIME TO GET THAT ARM OF YOURS READY (OR QUICKLY RUN OUT AND BUY AN ELECTRIC MIXER) AND WHISK THE ABSOLUTE ENDLESS FUCK OUT OF THE CREAM, WHICH AS I'VE MENTIONED IN OTHER PARTS OF THIS BOOK TAKES WAY LONGER THAN IT SHOULD, BUT DOES - TRUST ME - GET THERE IN THE END. THE CREAM SEEMINGLY OUT OF NOWHERE WILL FORM NICE THICK PEAKS, AT WHICH TIME YOU MAY NEED A SHOULDER RECONSTRUCTION, BUT IT'S ALSO A GREAT TIME TO FOLD THE CREAM INTO THE HORSE JOKE BOWL OF MASCARPONE FROM EARLIER.

NOW, SOME COFFEE IS NEEDED. HOWEVER YOU CHOOSE TO GET THERE IS UP TO YOU. I DON'T WANT TO HAVE TO GROW A BEARD AND TIE A TOP KNOT AND GET INTO A WHOLE BARISTA THING HERE ABOUT 'WHAT KIND OF FUCKEN COFFEE TO USE' 'CAUSE I DON'T REALLY GIVE A SPECIAL FUCK. JUST AS LONG AS IT'S 1½ CUPS OF STRONG BLACK COFFEE (AND NO, A SHITTY ICED COFFEE FROM THE SERVO WILL NOT DO THE TRICK, CHAMP).

ONCE YOU'VE NAVIGATED THAT JOURNEY, MAGELLAN, ADD THE REMAINING ¼ CUP OF SUGAR TO IT AND TIP THE SWEET COFFEE INTO A SHALLOW BOWL FOR COOL REASONS THAT IT NEEDS TO COOL OFF. COOL? ONCE IT'S TOO COOL FOR SCHOOL, STIR IN THE MARSALA OR FRANGELICO.

YOU RIFLING THROUGH YOUR CUPBOARD AND SUDDENLY FINDING A 22 CM SQUARE DISH IS FANTASTIC NEWS FOR US ALL RIGHT NOW, 'CAUSE WE WILL USE IT. SPREAD ABOUT A THIRD OF THE HORSE HIDER INTO THE BOTTOM OF THE DISH, THEN WITH YOUR HANDS OR TONGS IF YOU HAVE A GENTLE TOUCH, DIP THE BICKIES INTO THE COFFEE MIXTURE- DIP FAST 'CAUSE NEITHER THE BICKIES NOR THE COFFEE WILL LAST. THEN ARRANGE THEM OVER THE MASCARPONE UNTIL YOU'VE CREATED A LAYER.

NOW DUST OVER SOME COCOA WITH A SIEVE, COVER IT WITH HALF OF THE REMAINING HORSE HIDER AND ANOTHER LAYER OF COFFEE-DIPPED BICKIES FOLLOWED BY MORE COCOA POWDER. TOP ALL THAT WITH THE REMAINING CREAM MIXTURE, SMOOTH OUT THE TOP LAYER AND AGAIN DUST WITH MORE COCOA.

LAYERS OF GOODNESS

COCOA DUSTIN'
MASCARPONE
COCOA DUSTIN
COFFEE BICKIES
MASCARPONE
COCOA DUSTIN'
COFFEE BICKIES
THIN LAYER MASCARPONE

GIMME A BREAK
CELEBRATION
CAKE

Making someone an exciting looking cake – or any cake at all – is a daunting prospect for most, yet such a sweet gesture of love. Certainly, baking can be fucken tricky and fiddly shit that possibly only the brave and patient attempt. Well, it doesn't have to be that way, champion. With a couple of cheeky food-colouring manoeuvres and a borderline irresponsible amount of sugar, you'll be presenting the birthday personality with a cake so colourful and rad you'll be giving the rainbow a run for its money.

SERVES:
8–10
COOKING TIME:
about 1½ hours

HECTOMETER: 4/10

KEY:
Feed the Team | Kiddo friendly | Vego

INGREDIENTS

CAKE

- 125g UNSALTED BUTTER AT ROOM TEMP
- ¾ CUP CASTER SUGAR
- GRATED ZEST OF 1 LEMON
- 3 EGGS
- 2 CUPS SELF-RAISING FLOUR
- PINCH O' SALT
- ¼ CUP FULL CREAM MILK
- JUICE OF 1 LEMON
  (APPROX. ⅓ CUP LEMON JUICE)

- 4 DIFFERENT COLOURS OF FOOD DYE TO MAKE THE RAINBOW UNICORN CAKE OF YOUR DREAMS (OPTIONAL)

BUTTER CREAM ICING

- 1½-2 CUPS ICING SUGAR
- 125 G UNSALTED BUTTER AT ROOM TEMP
- ½ TEASPOON VANILLA ESSENCE
- 1 TABLESPOON FULL CREAM MILK

GEAR

- 22 CM CAKE TIN
- BAKING PAPER
- 2 MIXING BOWLS
- 4 SMALL BOWLS FOR COLOURING THE CAKE MIX (OPTIONAL)

PREHEAT THE OVEN TO 180°C FAN-FORCED (200°C CONVENTIONAL). GREASE AND LINE A 22CM ROUND CAKE TIN (OR WHATEVER KIND OF SHAPE YOU WANT).

IF YOU HAVE A CAKE MIXER OR ELECTRIC BEATER, THAT'S SUPER COOL FOR YOU. I DON'T, SO JULES AND I TEND TO USE A FORK AND THAT GOES FINE.

TO MAKE THE CAKE BATTER, COMBINE THE BUTTER, SUGAR AND LEMON ZEST. MIX THE SHIT OUT OF IT UNTIL IT CHANGES COLOUR A LITTLE AND BECOMES LIGHTER AND A BIT FLUFFY. THIS IS CALLED 'CREAMING' WHICH IS AN ODDLY UNSETTLING TERM, BUT NONETHELESS THE IDEA IS TO MIX IT UNTIL IT BECOMES... (WAIT FOR IT)
... THAT'S RIGHT, FUCKEN CREAMY.

EEEEEW.

ADD YOUR BUM NUTS/EGGS ONE AT A TIME, CONTINUING TO MIX THE FUCKEN FUCK OUT OF IT AFTER EACH IS INCORPORATED INTO THE MIXTURE.

LET'S INTRODUCE THE FLOUR IN TWO HALVES

SO, TO EXPLAIN: YA GONNA WANNA SIFT HALF THE FLOUR WITH A PINCH OF SALT INTO THE BOWL AND FOLD THAT INTO THE MIXTURE GENTLY.

THEN BUNG IN THE MILK AND MIX, THEN SIFT IN THE REST OF THE FLOUR AND COMBINE.

FINALLY, MIX IN YOUR LEMON JUICE.

EASE UP TURBO!!! DON'T THINK YOU'RE GONNA GET AWAY WITH SAVING TIME BY COMBINING THE LEMON JUICE AND THE MILK: THAT SHIT WILL FUCKEN CURDLE.

NOW, DEPENDING ON HOW LITTLE YOU GIVE A FUCK ABOUT MAKING THE CAKE LOOK EXCITING OR NOT (IE. YOU MIGHT JUST WANT A PLAIN CAKE), YOU CAN SIMPLY SPOON THE MIXTURE INTO THE TIN AND BUNG IT IN THE OVEN FOR 35-40 MINUTES OR UNTIL A SKEWER OR KNIFE INSERTED AT THE CENTRE COMES OUT CLEAN.

BUT HERE'S THE OPTIONAL EXTRA BIT IF YOU WANNA ADD A LITTLE MORE VISUAL EXCITEMENT TO THE EXERCISE. IT'S ACTUALLY NOT THAT HARD AND YOU CAN GO AS FUCKEN WILD AS YOU LIKE.

IF YOU WANT FOUR COLOURS IN THE CAKE, DIVIDE THE CAKE MIXTURE EVENLY INTO FOUR BOWLS, OR HOWEVER MANY COLOURS YOU'RE FEELING, REMBRANDT.

ADD A COUPLE OF DROPS OF DIFFERENT FOOD COLOURING TO EACH BOWL AND MIX UNTIL THE COLOUR IS AS VIBRANT AS YOU WANT.

YOU DON'T FUCKEN NEED MUCH OF THAT SHIT, FYI, SO GO EASY WITH THE FOOD DYE, AS A LITTLE GOES A BLOODY LONG WAY.
ALSO, MAYBE DON'T WEAR YOUR BRAND-NEW SLACKS AND CRISPY WHITE GOING-OUT SHIRT SINCE THEY COULD END UP LOOKING LIKE YOU HAD A PUNCH-ON WITH A BAG OF SKITTLES.

TRANSFER THE DIFFERENTLY COLOURED MIXTURES INTO THE CAKE TIN, A SPOONFUL OF ONE COLOUR AT A TIME. TRY NOT TO GET TOO MUCH OF THE SAME COLOUR IN ONE SPOT. IT DOESN'T HEAPS MATTER, THE ONLY REASON BEING IT WILL DOMINATE THE COLOUR MIX AND YOU POSSIBLY WON'T GET ASKED TO PARTICIPATE IN THE ARCHIBALD WITH YOUR MOSTLY GREEN ON ONE SIDE CAKE.

POW!

CONTINUE UNTIL ALL THE MIXTURE IS IN, THEN GIVE THE TIN A BIT OF A CHEEKY WIGGLE TO EVEN THE MIXTURE OUT.
YOU CAN LEAVE IT HERE... BUT DON'T, BECAUSE THE NEXT STEP IS SICK.

GRAB A CHOPSTICK, SKEWER, *HIGHLANDER* SWORD OR EVEN A BREADKNIFE TO GENTLY SWIRL THE BATTER IN A FIGURE OF EIGHT PATTERN OR WHATEVER DIRECTION TAKES YOU IN THE MOMENT TO CREATE A MARBLED EFFECT. BUT BEWARE IF YOU GET TOO CARRIED AWAY YOU'LL HAVE A SEWER-COLOURED CAKE ON YOUR HANDS.

IT'S NOT PARRAMATTA SPEEDWAY, IT'S A FANCY CAKE, SO KEEP THE HOT LAPS WITH THE STICK TO TWO OR THREE, YOU STILL WANT THE COLOURS TO BE SOMEWHAT SEPARATE OR IT WILL LOOK SHIT.

But also pretty funny.

FINALLY YOU CAN VINCENT VAN GO CHUCK IT IN THE OVEN FOR 35-40 MINUTES, CHECK WHETHER IT'S DONE WITH A SKEWER OR KNIFE AS MENTIONED EARLIER AND PLACE ON A COOLING RACK OR TRAY OR BALANCE IT ON YOUR HEAD.

ICING SUGA

VANILLA ESSENCE

MILK

Don't sweat if it's a little cracked on top, we will cover that with icing anyway.

ONCE THE CAKE IS COMPLETELY COOLED, IT'S TIME FOR THE ICING.

(DON'T ICE IT WHILE IT'S HOT, THE ICING WILL FUCKEN MELT AND DRIBBLE ALL OVER THE JOINT.)

VANILLA BUTTERCREAM ICING

SIFT THE ICING SUGAR INTO A BOWL, AND USING A FORK OR AN ELECTRIC BEATER MIX IN THE BUTTER UNTIL LIGHT AND FLUFFY.

ADD THE VANILLA ESSENCE AND ADD MILK AND COMBINE. IF THE ICING MIXTURE STILL SEEMS TOO UP-TIGHT/STIFF, YOU CAN ADD A LITTLE MORE MILK OR A FEW DROPS OF WATER UNTIL IT'S GOING AT THE PACE YOU WANT.

HOME STRETCH CHAMPION: SPREAD THE ICING OVER THE COOLED CAKE HOWEVER YOU LIKE – OVER THE TOP, ON THE TOP, AROUND THE SIDES.

BONUS ★ IDEA ★

IF YOUR PREVIOUS COLOURING-IN CARRY ON WASN'T ENOUGH, YOU CAN ALSO ADD A FEW DROPS OF A FIFTH COLOUR TO DYE THE ICING. YOU CAN EVEN SEPARATE A FEW TABLESPOONS OF ICING AND BUNG FOOD COLOURING INTO THAT, AND USING A SMALL PIPING BAG OR CHOPSTICK, WRITE SOME STUPID SENTENCE ON THE TOP OF THE WHITE ICING, CONGRATULATING SAID CHAMPION ON BEING JUST THAT.

GIVE THIS AMAZING COLOURFUL CAKE TO A BEAUTIFUL LEGEND WHO DESERVES A DOSE OF JOY AND LOVE TODAY.

Alternatively YOU CAN ALSO CHALLENGE THE LOCAL HOMOPHOBE BY HANDING IT TO THEM ALONG WITH A MIRROR SO THEY CAN TAKE A LOOK AT THEMSELVES WHILE THEY PRETEND NOT TO LOVE THE CAKE IN ALL ITS RAINBOW GLORY.

PARTY ON.

WAKE & DON'T BAKE ORANGE & LEMON CHEESECAKE

I have memories of eating cheesecake at a shitty shopping-centre café as a kid and trying to forget the word 'cheese' while I ate it. Definitely a little confused as to how it fucking had actual 'cheese' in it?, I was. I mean it does, but it's not the kind of cheese I was thinking of back then. I think I pictured a Kraft Single with sprinkles on it and a lit candle popped on top, or something. I've since learned how the magic happens there and I'm sure it helps that I'm not seven years old anymore, which is great news for us all, as otherwise this book would be full of ice cream and Fruit Loops recipes. No-bake cheesecake was Jules' idea, by the way – a ripper one it is too. The shit is so easy to make, particularly my way. I mean it when I say 'don't bake' . . . like you don't need to do.

SERVES:
8
COOKING TIME:
under 30 mins to not even cook;
resting time: 4+ hours

HECTOMETER: 3/10

KEY:

Cheap AF | Feed the Team | Kiddo Friendly | Low Stress | Vego

INGREDIENTS

CHEESE SINGLES AND ICE MAGIC (JUST KIDDING)

ACTUAL INGREDIENTS

1 ORANGE (HALF FOR JUICE, ONE FOR ZEST)
2 LEMONS (TWO FOR JUICE, ONE FOR ZEST)
200 G SCOTCH FINGER OR DIGESTIVE BICKIES
100 G BUTTER, PLUS EXTRA FOR GREASING
500 G CREAM CHEESE, AT ROOM TEMPERATURE (BLOCK FORM,
   NOT SPREADABLE)
140 G CASTER SUGAR
1 CUP THICKENED CREAM
1 TEASPOON GROUND DUTCH CINNAMON, OR JUST NORMAL SHIT

GEAR

20CM-ISH ROUND
   SPRINGFORM CAKE TIN

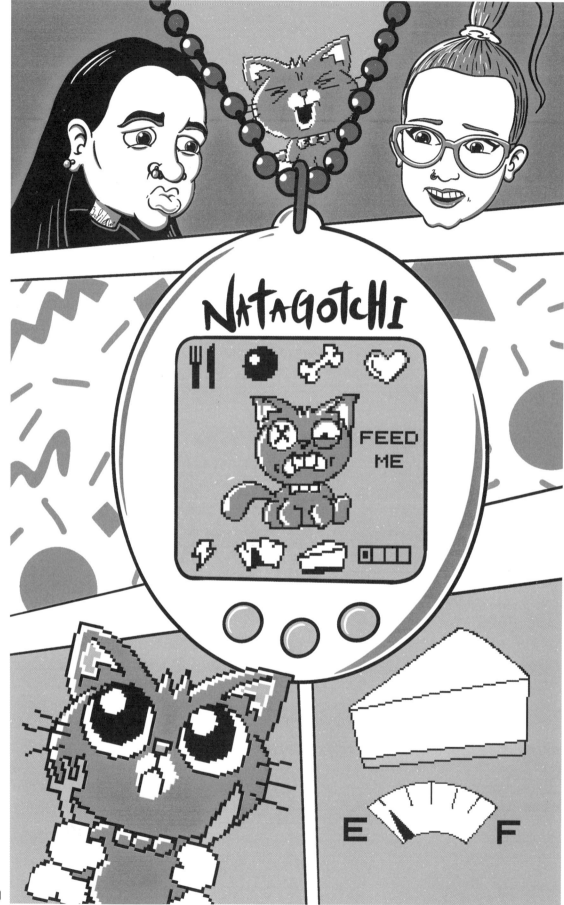

GIVE IT A GOOD PRESS FLAT AND WHACK IT IN THE FRIDGE FOR A MOMENT WHILE WE MAKE THE OTHER SHIT.

GRAB A BOWL AND AN ELECTRIC MIXER IF YOU HAVE ONE (THOUGH A WHISK IS FINE TOO),

AND WORK THE CREAM CHEESE APART AS YOU ADD THE SUGAR AND KINDA MAKE IT INTO A HEAVY PASTE.

IN A SECOND BOWL YOU'RE GONNA NEED TO WHIP THE CREAM.

BUT IF YOU GOTTA, YA GOTTA – I'VE FUCKEN DONE IT SO MANY TIMES, SO I FEEL YA.

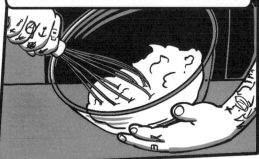

THIS ONE'S A SHIT JOB WITH A WHISK 'CAUSE IT TAKES LONGER THAN TRYING TO MOW THE FUCKEN GRASS WITH A PAIR OF SCISSORS.

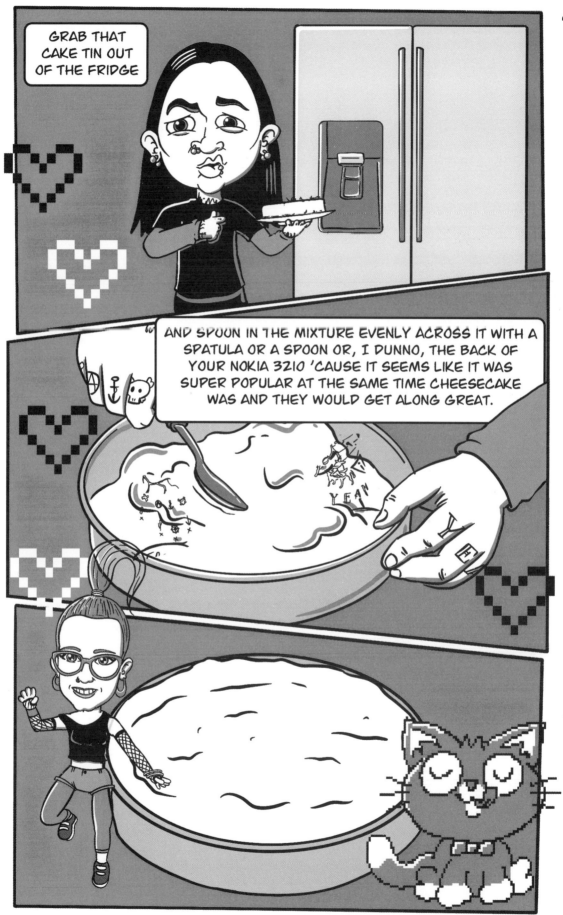

FROWNIE REVERSAL ORANGE CHOCOLATE BROWNIE

Brownies and orange-flavoured chocolate each have a reputation for being simultaneously awesome and indulgent, and, to be fair, a little old school, too. I remember orange chocolate being one of those things that would blow my little fucken mind as a kid, while pumping my lolly bag at the cinema full of enough Jaffas to frighten most parents. I have vivid memories of thinking that every time I ate chocolate with orange in it, those were probably some of the best times of my fucken life. So let's make memories and blow minds with the best fucken brownie in town.
(PS If you don't like orange chocolate, just don't put the orange in the brownie, lol.)

SERVES:
6–8 solid doses
COOKING TIME:
a bit over an hour

HECTOMETER: 4/10

KEY:
Comfort Food | Feed the Team | Kiddo Friendly | Vego

INGREDIENTS

- 1 large (or 2 small) oranges, zest only
- 200g butter
- 100g dark chocolate, go as dark or as less dark as you like, 70%+ seems to go pretty good, broken into pieces
- 1 cup plain flour
- 1/3 cup cocoa powder
- 1/2 teaspoon baking powder
- pinch of salt
- 1 cup caster sugar
- 1 cup brown sugar
- 4 eggs, lightly beaten
- 2 teaspoons vanilla bean paste or vanilla extract

IF YOU HAVE A PRECIOUS MICROPLANE (NOT A SMALL AIRCRAFT) OR GRATER, GRAB IT, AND ON THE FINEST SETTING ZEST THE ORANGE(S) INTO A BOWL.

OF COURSE, THIS RECIPE CAN WORK FOR *OTHER* TYPES OF BUTTER, PARTICULARLY ONES THAT MAY HAVE ACCIDENTALLY HAD SOME KIND OF FOLIAGE FLY THROUGH THE WINDOW INTO IT JUST WHEN YOU WERE TRYING TO COOK BUTTER, ON ITS OWN, SEEMINGLY FOR NO REASON.

SOOO, IF YOU'RE THAT WAY INCLINED FEEL FREE TO BE A LITTLE CREATIVE AND OF COURSE TRY TO REMEMBER THAT SOMETIMES EATING THINGS CAN BE A TOUCH MORE INTENSE THAN BREATHING THEM IN, IF YOU CATCH MY DRIFT.

Annie

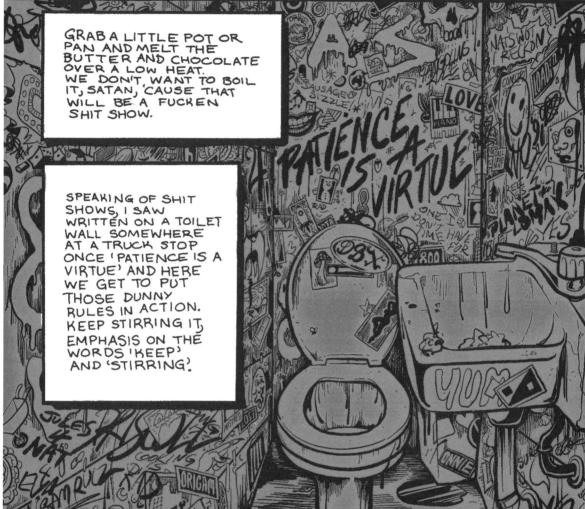

GRAB A LITTLE POT OR PAN AND MELT THE BUTTER AND CHOCOLATE OVER A LOW HEAT. WE DON'T WANT TO BOIL IT, SATAN, 'CAUSE THAT WILL BE A FUCKEN SHIT SHOW.

SPEAKING OF SHIT SHOWS, I SAW WRITTEN ON A TOILET WALL SOMEWHERE AT A TRUCK STOP ONCE 'PATIENCE IS A VIRTUE' AND HERE WE GET TO PUT THOSE DUNNY RULES IN ACTION. KEEP STIRRING IT, EMPHASIS ON THE WORDS 'KEEP' AND 'STIRRING'.

DON'T STOP BUT GENTLY BENTLEY, REMEMBERING EASY DOES IT AS WE CALMLY MELT BUTTER AND CHOCOLATE TOGETHER.

WHEN THAT SERENE MOMENT HAS ARRIVED WHERE THESE TWO INGREDIENTS ARE GETTING ALONG JUST FINE, IN WITH THE ORANGE ZEST, THEN SET ASIDE TO COOL OFF AMID A POSSIBLE CALMING BREEZE,
AND IF YOU HAVE A COMPACT DISC WITH A WHALE SONG PLAYING IN THE BACKGROUND, THAT MAY ALSO HELP.
HOTTEST HITS OF 2007
WHALE
SIFT YOUR FLOUR, COCOA AND BAKING POWDER INTO A BOWL WITH A CHEEKY PINCH OF SODIUM CHLORIDE.
WHEN I WAS A KID I THOUGHT I WAS A FUCKEN SCIENTIST AFTER I WORKED OUT THAT SODIUM CHLORIDE JUST MEANT SALT.
1kg
FLOUR
ADD IN THE SUGARS AND GIVE IT A GOOD MIX TOGETHER PLEASE AND THANK YOU. I DON'T KNOW HOW MANY RECIPE BOOKS YOU'VE READ THAT THANK YOU FOR DOING THE SHIT IN THEM, BUT THIS ONE DOES.

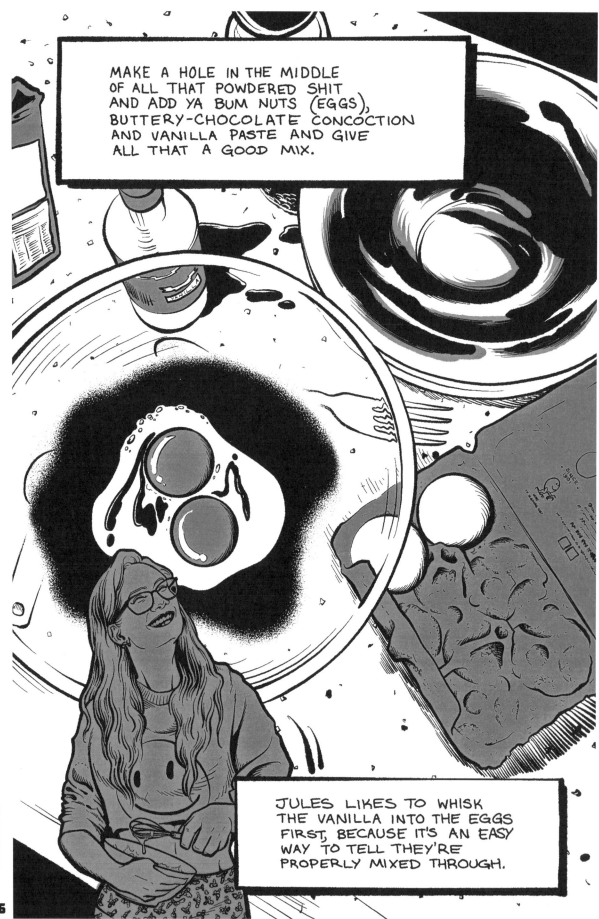

NOW WE'RE OFF TO THE RACES GROOVER. TIP ALL THAT RADNESS GENTLY INTO THE TRAY, SPREAD IT OUT EVEN STEPHEN AND BUNG IT IN THE OVEN FOR 45 MINUTES OR UNTIL JUST SET IN THE CENTRE.

A GOOD WAY TO TELL IS TO GIVE IT A GENTLE SHAKE — THE ULTIMATE BROWNIE CONSISTENCY IS COMPLETELY SET ON THE EDGES WITH A SLIGHT LIDDLE JIGGLE IN THE MIDDLE.

PAVLOVA THE PATIENCE CAKE

I mean, do I really need to say anything here? It's a pav, for fuck's sake. This is the *BMX Bandits* of cakes: chockers full of what I'm sure are Chrissytime memories of being surrounded by punishing relatives you wish you could escape, as well as bizarre and often overly expressive fruit arrangements on what is more or less a giant meringue. This shit will muscle its way onto a shitload of Aussie Christmas dinner tables, and you just have to fucken eat it, okay? So let's make one that's actually so sick it probably wears a backwards Monster Energy hat and does backflips on a jet ski.

SERVES:
6–8
COOKING TIME:
a few hours

HECTOMETER: 6/10

KEY:
Feed the Team | Impress the Judges | Vego

INGREDIENTS

6 EGG WHITES FROM XL EGGS (FROM A 700G BOX OF A DOZEN)
* IF YOU'RE USING SMALL EGGS, (SAY FROM A 550G DOZEN) THEN YOU NEED TO USE ANOTHER EGG WHITE.
1½ CUPS (330 G) CASTER SUGAR, PLUS 1 TEASPOON FOR CREAM
2 TEASPOONS CORNFLOUR
1 TEASPOON WHITE VINEGAR
300 ML THICKENED CREAM
1 TEASPOON VANILLA EXTRACT OR VANILLA BEAN PASTE
FRUIT, TO SERVE
(BERRIES RULE BUT YOU CAN CHOOSE YOUR ADVENTURE)

CHOOSE YOUR FRUIT ADVENTURE

YOU'RE THE CHAMPION OF THE STORY!
CHOOSE FROM 22 POSSIBLE ENDINGS

FRUITS FOR THE PAVLOVA PLANET

BY NAT'S WHAT I RECKON

ILLUSTRATED BY GLENNO

LET'S JUST SAY THAT PAVS ARE A LITTLE LIKE SNOWFLAKES — THEY ARE DELICATE AND HAVE A RANGE OF STRUCTURAL INTEGRITY ISSUES IN THEIR LIVES, JUST LIKE WE ALL DO. I'M NOT SAYING YOU'RE A PAVLOVA, BUT MAYBE WE CAN LEARN SOMETHING FROM THIS CALORIE-DENSE DESSERT TODAY.

PREHEAT YOUR OVEN TO 150°C FLAN-FORCED (170°C NORMAL NATHAN STYLE), AND LINE A BAKING TRAY WITH BAKING PAPER.

SEPARATE YOUR EGG WHITES FROM THE YOLKS. THERE'S A WHOLE BOOK IN EXPLAINING HOW TO DO THAT IN SO MANY WAYS, SO LET ME MAKE IT SIMPLE FOR YA IF YOU'RE NOT GREAT AT IT: WASH YOUR FUCKEN GRUBBY HIGH-FIVIN' HANDS, CRACK THE EGGS ONE AT A TIME INTO ONE HAND YOU'RE HOLDING OVER A BOWL AND SEPARATE YOUR FINGERS JUST ENOUGH TO LET THE WHITE FALL THROUGH INTO THE BOWL. KEEP THE YOLKS FOR SOME OTHER SHIT. I DUNNO ... MAYBE MAKE A YOLK HAT OUT OF THEM? OR TAKE THEM TO AN ANNOYING YOLK FESTIVAL AND BUY IT AN ITCHY PAIR OF HEMP PANTS WITH HEAPS OF SMALL MIRRORS ON THAT MAKE THEM LOOK LIKE A FAILED MAGICIAN? THE OPTIONS ARE ENDLESS.

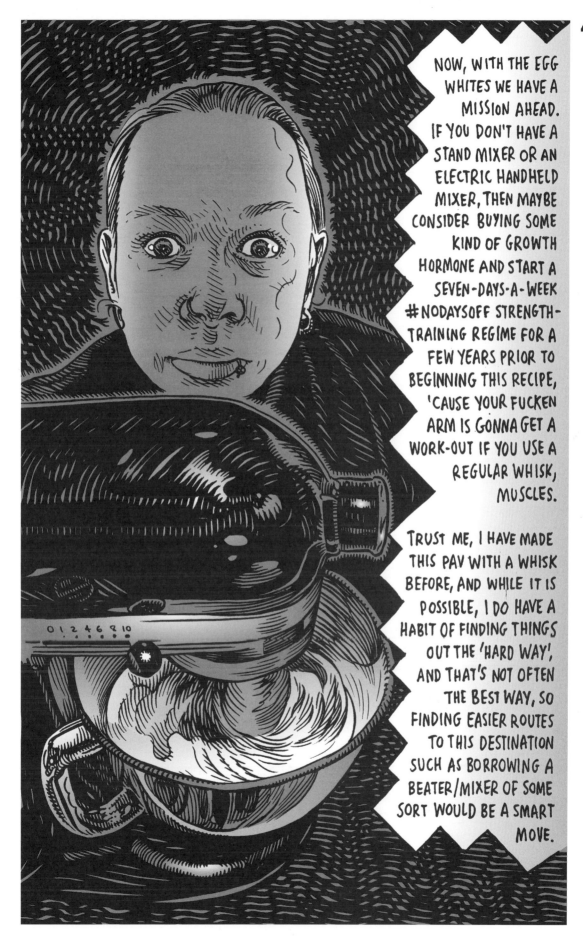

NOW, WITH THE EGG WHITES WE HAVE A MISSION AHEAD. IF YOU DON'T HAVE A STAND MIXER OR AN ELECTRIC HANDHELD MIXER, THEN MAYBE CONSIDER BUYING SOME KIND OF GROWTH HORMONE AND START A SEVEN-DAYS-A-WEEK #NODAYSOFF STRENGTH-TRAINING REGIME FOR A FEW YEARS PRIOR TO BEGINNING THIS RECIPE, 'CAUSE YOUR FUCKEN ARM IS GONNA GET A WORK-OUT IF YOU USE A REGULAR WHISK, MUSCLES.

TRUST ME, I HAVE MADE THIS PAV WITH A WHISK BEFORE, AND WHILE IT IS POSSIBLE, I DO HAVE A HABIT OF FINDING THINGS OUT THE 'HARD WAY', AND THAT'S NOT OFTEN THE BEST WAY, SO FINDING EASIER ROUTES TO THIS DESTINATION SUCH AS BORROWING A BEATER/MIXER OF SOME SORT WOULD BE A SMART MOVE.

WHATEVER OPTION YOU'VE GONE FOR, YOU'RE GUNNA NEED TO WHISK/BEAT/HARD WAY THOSE EGG WHITES INTO SOFT PEAKS. GRADUALLY ADD THE SUGAR 1 TABLESPOON AT A TIME UNTIL YOUR ARM HAS FUCKEN CALLED THE COPS ON YOU, THEN IN GOES THE CORN FLOUR AND VINEGAR IN THE SAME MANNER. KEEP WHISKING TILL ALL THE FUCKEN BLOODY SUGAR HAS DISSOLVED.

IF YOU'RE WONDERING WHETHER YOUR BIG WHITE BOWL OF CALORIE CLOUDS HAS REACHED THIS STAGE, THEN USE YOUR FINGERS TO SQUEEZE A LITTLE BETWEEN THEM AND SEE WHETHER IT FEELS SANDY OR NOT, IT SHOULD'NT.

SPOON YOUR EFFORT INTO THE CENTRE OF THE PREPARED BAKING TRAY, USING A FORKLIFT, OR IF YOU DON'T HAVE ONE OF THOSE LYING AROUND THEN THE BACK OF A SPOON WILL HAVE TO DO IN ORDER TO SHAPE IT INTO A THING.

YOU WANT TO MAKE THIS PILE OF FLUFF LOOK LIKE A SHAPE THAT RESEMBLES SOMETHING ALONG THE LINES OF A SERIOUSLY DEEP DISH LARGE PIZZA. I SUPPOSE LIKE ALL FOOD THAT YOU CREATE, IT'S MODERATELY CONCEPTUAL SO THERE IS NO RIGHT OR WRONG WAY TO SHAPE IT SINCE IT DOESN'T REALLY AFFECT THE FLAVOUR. I LIKE TO IMAGINE THE CHEAP SUPERMARKET MUD CAKE KINDA SHAPE AND GO FOR THAT ... SEEMS TO WORK WELL.

INDEX

A

apples: Die, Shitty Frozen Apple Pie! 386–95

aquafaba: vegan mayo, 363, 364

asparagus: Roast Veggies like a Bloody Champion, 340–55

avocados

(Not even shit) Rad Salad, 368–77

Ceviche on the Beach, 226–35

Chilli Con Can't be Fucked Quesadillas, 14–21

guacamole, 15–16, 87, 90–1

Pulled Pork Taco Night, 86–93

B

bacon *See also* pancetta; speck

The Creamy Mushroom, Bacon and White Wine Situation (pasta), 76–85

End of Days Bolognese, 56–65

Rice Rice Baby, 124–33

basil

Gimme the Fritz (zucchini fritters), 320–9

Pizza Party, 94–115

Quarantine Sauce V2, 330–7

BBQ-rious Pork Ribs with Indoor Corn and Rosemary Sweet Potato Fries, 66–75

bechamel, 143, 148–50

beef (mince)

Chilli Con Can't be Fucked Quesadillas, 14–21

End of Days Bolognese, 56–65

Straight to the Pool Room Rissoles, 48–55

beef (shin): Forgive Me for I Have Shins Osso Buco with Couscous and Yoghurt, 22–9

beef (stewing): Me, Myself and Guinness Pie, 30–47

beef stock

Forgive Me for I Have Shins Osso Buco with Couscous and Yoghurt, 22–9

Lamb Moussaka Therapy, 142–53

Sacrificial Lamb Rack, 162–71

Self Pie-solation Shepherd's Pie, 134–41

Shanks 4 Comin' Lamb Shanks with Mash, 154–61

beer

Me, Myself and Guinness Pie, 30–47

Pork 'Yeah' Belly, 116–23

beetroots: Roast Veggies like a Bloody Champion, 340–55

black beans *See also* pinto beans

Pulled Pork Taco Night, 86–93

Bond Eye Chicken Burger, 196–203

breadcrumbs

Lamb Moussaka Therapy, 142–53

Straight to the Pool Room Rissoles, 48–55

breadcrumbs (Panko)

Chicken Parmy, 188–95

Zero Fucks Mac 'n' Cheese, 246–51

breads: Go Focaccia Yourself, 378–83

brownies: Frownie Reversal Orange Chocolate Brownie, 420–9

brussels sprouts: Roast Veggies like a Bloody Champion, 340–55

Burgers: Bond Eye Chicken Burger, 196–203

buttermilk: The (Chicken) Wings of Love, 210–17

C

cabbage (red): Incidentally Vegan Street Coleslaw, 362–7

cabbage (white)

Incidentally Vegan Street Coleslaw, 362–7

Surf and Turf Mie Goreng, 218–25

Cakes: Gimme a Break Celebration Cake, 402–7

capsicums

Chilli Con Can't be Fucked Quesadillas, 14–21

Crowd Goes Mild Curry, 172–9

Spicy Pants Shakshuka, 262–9

carrots

Incidentally Vegan Street Coleslaw, 362–7

Roast Veggies like a Bloody Champion, 340–55

Vegenator 2: Judgement Tray Lasagne, 296–311

Ceviche on the Beach, 226–35

cheesecake: Wake and Don't Bake Orange and Lemon Cheesecake, 408–19

cheese (cheddar)

Chilli Con Can't be Fucked Quesadillas, 14–21

Self Pie-solation Shepherd's Pie, 134–41

Zero Fucks Mac 'n' Cheese, 246–51

cheese (goat's): (Not even shit) Rad Salad, 368–77

cheese (kefalograviera): Lamb Moussaka Therapy, 142–53

chicken breast

Bond Eye Chicken Burger, 196–203

Chicken Parmy, 188–95

chicken stock

Chilli, Pumpkin and Mushroom Rhys-otto, 280–7

Crowd Goes Mild Curry, 172–9

The Cure (sweet potato and pumpkin soup), 270–9

End of Days Bolognese, 56–65

Honey Bastard Chicken, 204–9

Pork 'Yeah' Belly, 116–23

Pulled Pork Taco Night, 86–93

Quarantine Sauce V2, 330–7

Red Curry Sweet Potato Soup, 288–95

Vegenator 2: Judgement Tray Lasagne, 296–311

chicken thighs

Crowd Goes Mild Curry, 172–9

Honey Bastard Chicken, 204–9

Surf and Turf Mie Goreng, 218–25

chicken (whole): Winner, Winner Roast Chicken Dinner, 180–7

chicken wings: The (Chicken) Wings of Love, 210–17

chickpea juice *See* aquafaba

chickpeas

Forgive Me for I Have Shins Osso Buco with Couscous and Yoghurt, 22–9

Incidentally Vegan Street Coleslaw, 362–7

Chilli, Pumpkin and Mushroom Rhys-otto, 280–7

Chilli Con Can't be Fucked Quesadillas, 14–21

chillies (bird's eye)

Chilli, Pumpkin and Mushroom Rhys-otto, 280–7

chilli sauce, 197, 199

Gnocch-on or Fuck Off Chilli Tomato Gnocchi, 312–19
Quarantine Sauce V2, 330–7
chillies (red)
chilli sauce, 181, 183, 185
Crowd Goes Mild Curry, 172–9
Gimme the Fritz (zucchini fritters), 320–9
Red Curry Sweet Potato Soup, 288–95
Sacrificial Lamb Rack, 162–71
Spicy Pants Shakshuka, 262–9
chipotle
Chilli Con Can't be Fucked Quesadillas, 14–21
chipotle mayo, 211, 212
chocolate (dark): Frownie Reversal Orange Chocolate Brownie, 420–9
cocoa powder
Frownie Reversal Orange Chocolate Brownie, 420–9
Jim's Tirameezoo, 396–401
coconut cream: Crowd Goes Mild Curry, 172–9
coconut milk: Red Curry Sweet Potato Soup, 288–95
coffee: Jim's Tirameezoo, 396–401
coriander
Ceviche on the Beach, 226–35
Chilli Con Can't be Fucked Quesadillas, 14–21
Fish Cakes, 236–45
Pulled Pork Taco Night, 86–93
Red Curry Sweet Potato Soup, 288–95
Spicy Pants Shakshuka, 262–9
corn
BBQ-rious Pork Ribs with Indoor Corn and Rosemary Sweet Potato Fries, 66–75
Rice Rice Baby, 124–33
corn chips: Ceviche on the Beach, 226–35
cornflour: The (Chicken) Wings of Love, 210–17
couscous: Forgive Me for I Have Shins Osso Buco with Couscous and Yoghurt, 22–9
cream
The Creamy Mushroom, Bacon and White Wine Situation (pasta), 76–85
Self Pie-solation Shepherd's Pie, 134–41
cream (thickened)
Jim's Tirameezoo, 396–401
Pavlova the Patience Cake, 430–7
Wake and Don't Bake Orange and Lemon Cheesecake, 408–19
cream cheese: Wake and Don't Bake Orange and Lemon Cheesecake, 408–19
The Creamy Mushroom, Bacon and White Wine Situation (pasta), 76–85
crème fraîche: Honey Bastard Chicken, 204–9
Crowd Goes Mild Curry, 172–9
cucumbers (Lebanese)
Ceviche on the Beach, 226–35
(Not even shit) Rad Salad, 368–77
quick pickle, 87, 91
The Cure (sweet potato and pumpkin soup), 270–9
curries: Crowd Goes Mild Curry, 172–9
curry pastes, 289, 291–2

D

deep frying temperatures, 216
Die, Shitty Frozen Apple Pie! 386–95

dips
chipotle mayo, 211, 212
Pulled Pork Taco Night, 86–93
dough: Pizza Party, 94–115
dressings, 372–5

E

eggplants: Lamb Moussaka Therapy, 142–53
eggs
Chicken Parmy, 188–95
chipotle mayo, 211, 212
Frownie Reversal Orange Chocolate Brownie, 420–9
Jim's Tirameezoo, 396–401
Rice Rice Baby, 124–33
Spicy Pants Shakshuka, 262–9
Spinach, Ricotta and better with Feta Pie, 252–61
End of Days Bolognese, 56–65

F

feta
Spicy Pants Shakshuka, 262–9
Spinach, Ricotta and better with Feta Pie, 252–61
Vegenator 2: Judgement Tray Lasagne, 296–311
fish See also kingfish
Ceviche on the Beach, 226–35
Fish Cakes, 236–45
focaccia: Go Focaccia Yourself, 378–83
Forgive Me for I Have Shins Osso Buco with Couscous and Yoghurt, 22–9
freezing tips for sauces, 65
French shallots
Chilli, Pumpkin and Mushroom Rhys-otto, 280–7
Red Curry Sweet Potato Soup, 288–95
Rice Rice Baby, 124–33
Sacrificial Lamb Rack, 162–71
fries: Rosemary Sweet Potato Fries, 71
fritters: Gimme the Fritz (zucchini fritters), 320–9
Frownie Reversal Orange Chocolate Brownie, 420–9
fruit: Pavlova the Patience Cake, 430–7

G

galangal: Red Curry Sweet Potato Soup, 288–95
garlic
Chilli, Pumpkin and Mushroom Rhys-otto, 280–7
cooking it right, 146
The Creamy Mushroom, Bacon and White Wine Situation (pasta), 76–85
Crowd Goes Mild Curry, 172–9
The Cure (sweet potato and pumpkin soup), 270–9
Forgive Me for I Have Shins Osso Buco with Couscous and Yoghurt, 22–9
garlic yoghurt, 315, 317
Gnocch-on or Fuck Off Chilli Tomato Gnocchi, 312–19
Lamb Moussaka Therapy, 142–53
Me, Myself and Guinness Pie, 30–47
Pulled Pork Taco Night, 86–93
Quarantine Sauce V2, 330–7
Red Curry Sweet Potato Soup, 288–95
roasting tips, 353–4
Roast Veggies like a Bloody Champion, 340–55
Sacrificial Lamb Rack, 162–71
Self Pie-solation Shepherd's Pie, 134–41
Shanks 4 Comin' Lamb Shanks with Mash, 154–61

Spicy Pants Shakshuka, 262–9
Spinach, Ricotta and better with Feta Pie, 252–61
Surf and Turf Mie Goreng, 218–25
Vegenator 2: Judgement Tray Lasagne, 296–311
Zero Fucks Mac 'n' Cheese, 246–51
Get Fucked Roast Potatoes, 356–61
Gimme a Break Celebration Cake, 402–7
Gimme the Fritz (zucchini fritters), 320–9
ginger
    Crowd Goes Mild Curry, 172–9
    The Cure (sweet potato and pumpkin soup), 270–9
    Fish Cakes, 236–45
    Forgive Me for I Have Shins Osso Buco with
        Couscous and Yoghurt, 22–9
Gnocch-on or Fuck Off Chilli Tomato Gnocchi, 312–19
Go Focaccia Yourself, 378–83
gravy: Winner, Winner Roast Chicken Dinner, 187
green beans: Fish Cakes, 236–45
guacamole, 15–16, 87, 90–1

H

haloumi: Gimme the Fritz (zucchini fritters), 320–9
ham: Rice Rice Baby, 124–33
hokkien noodles: Surf and Turf Mie Goreng, 218–25
Honey Bastard Chicken, 204–9

I

Incidentally Vegan Street Coleslaw, 356–61

J

jalapeño peppers
    Ceviche on the Beach, 226–35
    Pulled Pork Taco Night, 86–93
jus, 169 See also gravy

K

kecap manis: Surf and Turf Mie Goreng, 218–25
ketchup: BBQ-rious Pork Ribs with Indoor Corn and
    Rosemary Sweet Potato Fries, 66–75
kingfish: Ceviche on the Beach, 226–35
kitchen kit and utensils (gotta haves), 5–7
knife know-hows, 8–11

L

lamb mince
    Lamb Moussaka Therapy, 142–53
    Self Pie-solation Shepherd's Pie, 134–41
lamb rack
    frenching technique, 166
    Sacrificial Lamb Rack, 162–71
lamb shanks: Shanks 4 Comin' Lamb Shanks with
    Mash, 154–61
lasagne: Vegenator 2: Judgement Tray Lasagne,
    296–311
leeks
    The Cure (sweet potato and pumpkin soup), 270–9
    Red Curry Sweet Potato Soup, 288–95
lemongrass: Red Curry Sweet Potato Soup, 288–95
lemons
    chilli sauce, 181, 183, 185
    Gimme a Break Celebration Cake, 402–7
    Gimme the Fritz (zucchini fritters), 320–9
    Wake and Don't Bake Orange and Lemon
        Cheesecake, 408–19

lentils: Vegenator 2: Judgement Tray Lasagne,
    296–311
lime leaves (makrut)
    Fish Cakes, 226–35
    Red Curry Sweet Potato Soup, 288–95
limes
    Ceviche on the Beach, 226–35
    chipotle mayo, 211, 212
    juicing tip, 240
    Surf and Turf Mie Goreng, 218–25

M

marinades, 181, 183
marsala: Jim's Tirameezoo, 396–401
mascarpone: Jim's Tirameezoo, 396–401
mayonnaise, 197, 200
    chipotle mayo, 211, 212
    vegan mayo, 363, 364
Me, Myself and Guinness Pie, 30–47
meat thermometer, 167–8, 216, 217
meringue: Pavlova the Patience Cake, 430–7
milk
    bechamel, 248–9
    End of Days Bolognese, 56–65
    Quarantine Sauce V2, 330–7
    Self Pie-solation Shepherd's Pie, 134–41
    Shanks 4 Comin' Lamb Shanks with Mash,
        154–61
    Vegenator 2: Judgement Tray Lasagne, 296–311
    Zero Fucks Mac 'n' Cheese, 246–51
mozzarella
    Chicken Parmy, 188–95
    Pizza Party, 94–115
    Vegenator 2: Judgement Tray Lasagne, 296–311
    Zero Fucks Mac 'n' Cheese, 246–51
mushrooms
    Chilli, Pumpkin and Mushroom Rhys-otto, 280–7
    The Creamy Mushroom, Bacon and White Wine
        Situation (pasta), 76–85
mustard (Dijon)
    chipotle mayo, 211, 212
    Honey Bastard Chicken, 204–9
    Incidentally Vegan Street Coleslaw, 362–7
    Zero Fucks Mac 'n' Cheese, 246–51

N

no-bake desserts
    Jim's Tirameezoo, 396–401
    Wake and Don't Bake Orange and Lemon
        Cheesecake, 408–19
noodles: Surf and Turf Mie Goreng, 218–25
(Not even shit) Rad Salad, 368–77

O

onions, 353 See also French shallots
    Quarantine Sauce V2, 330–7
    Roast Veggies like a Bloody Champion, 340–55
    Spicy Pants Shakshuka, 262–9
    Winner, Winner Roast Chicken Dinner, 180–7
oranges
    Frownie Reversal Orange Chocolate Brownie, 420–9
    Wake and Don't Bake Orange and Lemon
        Cheesecake, 408–19
    Winner, Winner Roast Chicken Dinner, 180–7

P

pancetta: End of Days Bolognese, 56–65
pantry staples, 2–4
parboiling tips for vegetables, 342
parmesan
    Chicken Parmy, 188–95
    Chilli, Pumpkin and Mushroom Rhys-otto, 280–7
    Self Pie-solation Shepherd's Pie, 134–41
    Vegenator 2: Judgement Tray Lasagne, 296–311
    Zero Fucks Mac 'n' Cheese, 246–51
parsley
    Honey Bastard Chicken, 204–9
    Spicy Pants Shakshuka, 262–9
parsnips: Roast Veggies like a Bloody Champion,
    340–55
pasta
    The Creamy Mushroom, Bacon and White Wine
        Situation (pasta), 76–85
    End of Days Bolognese, 56–65
    Quarantine Sauce V2, 330–7
    Vegenator 2: Judgement Tray Lasagne, 296–311
    Zero Fucks Mac 'n' Cheese, 246–51
pastry, blind baking tips, 393
pastry (filo): Spinach, Ricotta and better with Feta Pie,
    252–61
pastry (puff): Me, Myself and Guinness Pie, 30–47
pastry (shortcrust)
    cooking tips, 42
    Die, Shitty Frozen Apple Pie! 386–95
    Me, Myself and Guinness Pie, 30–47
Pavlova the Patience Cake, 430–7
peaches: (Not even shit) Rad Salad, 368–77
pears: Die, Shitty Frozen Apple Pie! 386–95
peas
    Rice Rice Baby, 124–33
    Self Pie-solation Shepherd's Pie, 134–41
pickles, 87, 91
pies
    Die, Shitty Frozen Apple Pie! 386–95
    Me, Myself and Guinness Pie, 30–47
    Self Pie-solation Shepherd's Pie, 134–41
    Spinach, Ricotta and better with Feta Pie, 252–61
pine nuts: (Not even shit) Rad Salad, 368–77
pinto beans
    Chilli Con Can't be Fucked Quesadillas, 14–21
    Pulled Pork Taco Night, 86–93
Pizza Party, 94–115
pork mince: End of Days Bolognese, 56–65
pork ribs: BBQ-rious Pork Ribs with Indoor Corn and
    Rosemary Sweet Potato Fries, 66–75
pork shoulder: Pulled Pork Taco Night, 86–93
Pork 'Yeah' Belly, 116–23
potatoes
    Get Fucked Roast Potatoes, 356–61
    Gnocch-on or Fuck Off Chilli Tomato Gnocchi,
        312–19
    Lamb Moussaka Therapy, 142–53
    Roast Veggies like a Bloody Champion, 340–55
    roasting tips, 343–7
    Self Pie-solation Shepherd's Pie, 134–41
    Shanks 4 Comin' Lamb Shanks with Mash, 154–61
prawns: Surf and Turf Mie Goreng, 218–25
prosciutto: Pizza Party, 94–115
Pulled Pork Taco Night, 86–93

pumpkin (butternut)
    Chilli, Pumpkin and Mushroom Rhys-otto, 280–7
    The Cure (sweet potato and pumpkin soup), 270–9
    Red Curry Sweet Potato Soup, 288–95
    Roast Veggies like a Bloody Champion, 340–55
    roasting tips, 348–9
    Vegenator 2: Judgement Tray Lasagne, 296–311

Q

Quarantine Sauce V2, 330–7
quesadillas: Chilli Con Can't be Fucked Quesadillas,
    14–21

R

raspberries: Die, Shitty Frozen Apple Pie! 386–95
Red Curry Sweet Potato Soup, 288–95
red wine
    Lamb Moussaka Therapy, 142–53
    Quarantine Sauce V2, 330–7
    Sacrificial Lamb Rack, 162–71
    Shanks 4 Comin' Lamb Shanks with Mash, 154–61
    Vegenator 2: Judgement Tray Lasagne, 296–311
rice (carnaroli or arborio): Chilli, Pumpkin and
    Mushroom Rhys-otto, 280–7
rice (white)
    Crowd Goes Mild Curry, 172–9
    Rice Rice Baby 124–33
rice flour: Fish Cakes, 236–45
Rice Rice Baby, 124–33
ricotta
    Spinach, Ricotta and better with Feta Pie, 252–61
    Vegenator 2: Judgement Tray Lasagne, 296–311
risotto: Chilli, Pumpkin and Mushroom Rhys-otto,
    280–7
rissoles: Straight to the Pool Room Rissoles, 48–55
Roast Veggies like a Bloody Champion, 340–55
roasting tips for root vegetables, 349–51, 354–5
roasting tips for vegetables, 351–2
roasts
    Sacrificial Lamb Rack, 162–71
    Winner, Winner Roast Chicken Dinner, 180–7
rocket: (Not even shit) Rad Salad, 368–77
rosemary: BBQ-rious Pork Ribs with Indoor Corn and
    Rosemary Sweet Potato Fries, 71
rubs, 67

S

Sacrificial Lamb Rack, 162–71
safety tips for frying, 216
salads: Incidentally Vegan Street Coleslaw, 362–7
sauces *See also* dips; dressings; mayonnaise
    BBQ sauce, 67, 70
    chilli sauce, 197, 199
    chilli tomato sauce, 313, 316
    pizza sauce, 95, 98–9
    Quarantine Sauce V2, 330–7
savoiardi biscuits: Jim's Tirameezoo, 396–401
schnitzels: Chicken Parmy, 188–95
scotch fingers: Wake and Don't Bake Orange and
    Lemon Cheesecake, 408–19
Self Pie-solation Shepherd's Pie, 134–41
shakshuka: Spicy Pants Shakshuka, 262–9
Shanks 4 Comin' Lamb Shanks with Mash, 154–61
shrimp paste: Red Curry Sweet Potato Soup, 288–95

slow cooks
    Forgive Me for I Have Shins Osso Buco with
        Couscous and Yoghurt, 22–9
    Shanks 4 Comin' Lamb Shanks with Mash, 154–61
soups
    The Cure (sweet potato and pumpkin soup), 270–9
    Red Curry Sweet Potato Soup, 288–95
sour cream: Honey Bastard Chicken, 204–9
speck: Rice Rice Baby, 124–33
spices
    BBQ-rious Pork Ribs with Indoor Corn and
        Rosemary Sweet Potato Fries, 66–75
    Bond Eye Chicken Burger, 196–203
    Chicken Parmy, 188–95
    The (Chicken) Wings of Love, 210–17
    Chilli Con Can't be Fucked Quesadillas, 14–21
    chilli sauce, 181, 183, 185
    Crowd Goes Mild Curry, 172–9
    Forgive Me for I Have Shins Osso Buco with
        Couscous and Yoghurt, 22–9
    Lamb Moussaka Therapy, 142–53
    Pulled Pork Taco Night, 86–93
    Red Curry Sweet Potato Soup, 288–95
    Spicy Pants Shakshuka, 262–9
spinach
    Spinach, Ricotta and better with Feta Pie, 252–61
    Vegenator 2: Judgement Tray Lasagne, 296–311
spring onions
    The Creamy Mushroom, Bacon and White Wine
        Situation (pasta), 76–85
    Spinach, Ricotta and better with Feta Pie, 252–61
stews: Forgive Me for I Have Shins Osso Buco with
    Couscous and Yoghurt, 22–9
stout: Self Pie-solation Shepherd's Pie, 134–41
Straight to the Pool Room Rissoles, 48–55
Surf and Turf Mie Goreng, 218–25
sweet potatoes
    BBQ-rious Pork Ribs with Indoor Corn and
        Rosemary Sweet Potato Fries, 66–75
    The Cure (sweet potato and pumpkin soup), 270–9
    Red Curry Sweet Potato Soup, 288–95
    Roast Veggies like a Bloody Champion, 368–83
    Sacrificial Lamb Rack, 162–71

T

tacos: Pulled Pork Taco Night, 86–93
temperature chart for lamb, 168
tiramisu: Jim's Tirameezoo, 396–401
tomato paste
    Chilli Con Can't be Fucked Quesadillas, 14–21
    End of Days Bolognese, 56–65

Lamb Moussaka Therapy, 142–53
    Pulled Pork Taco Night, 86–93
    Quarantine Sauce V2, 330–7
    Vegenator 2: Judgement Tray Lasagne, 296–311
tomatoes (fresh)
    Ceviche on the Beach, 226–35
    Chilli Con Can't be Fucked Quesadillas, 14–21
    Quarantine Sauce V2, 330–7
    quick pickle, 87, 91
tomatoes (tin)
    Crowd Goes Mild Curry, 172–9
    Forgive Me for I Have Shins Osso Buco with
        Couscous and Yoghurt, 22–9
    Gnocch-on or Fuck Off Chilli Tomato Gnocchi,
        312–19
    Lamb Moussaka Therapy, 142–53
    Pizza Party, 94–5
    Pulled Pork Taco Night, 86–93
    Spicy Pants Shakshuka, 262–9
    Vegenator 2: Judgement Tray Lasagne, 296–311
tortillas: Chilli Con Can't be Fucked Quesadillas,
    14–21

V

veal (shin): Forgive Me for I Have Shins Osso Buco
    with Couscous and Yoghurt, 22–9
Vegenator 2: Judgement Tray Lasagne, 296–311
vegetables: Roast Veggies like a Bloody Champion,
    340–55

W

Wake and Don't Bake Orange and Lemon
    Cheesecake, 408–19
white wine
    Chilli, Pumpkin and Mushroom Rhys-otto,
        280–7
    The Creamy Mushroom, Bacon and White Wine
        Situation (pasta), 76–85
    Winner, Winner Roast Chicken Dinner, 180–7

Y

yoghurt
    Forgive Me for I Have Shins Osso Buco with
        Couscous and Yoghurt, 22–9
    garlic yoghurt, 315, 317
    Yogo Blob, 173, 177

Z

Zero Fucks Mac 'n' Cheese, 246–51
zucchinis: Gimme the Fritz, 320–9

ACKNOWLEDGEMENTS

This book was written on unceded Gadigal Land. I acknowledge that Aboriginal and Torres Strait Islander people are the traditional custodians of this stolen land and pay my respects to Elders past and present.

Shit, I have levels of gratitude I can't begin to properly express, though I will bloody try. THANK YOU AF to my ridiculously talented artist mates: Onnie, Bunkwaa, Glenno and Warrick – mates, from the bottom of my silly heart – I thank you for sharing your mind-blowing talents to help turn my sweary words into incredible works of art.

Big thanks to all my legendary mates who helped me test out my recipes and see if my instructions were a bit on the piss. I bloody love ya's to bits, thanks and see ya's on the discord later. Warren Mendes and Hendrik Max, you bloody magical chef champions, thanks for helping me work out some kick-arse dishes and for double-checking my home-cooked carry-on for bung notes.

Izzy, Clive, Adam and PRH, holy shit you're absolute legends for backing me in my wild book endeavours. I wouldn't be here without you.

Andrew, Julie, Tobie and Tom, thanks for looking out for me, for reading insanely long contracts that probably make your eyes want to fall out of your poor fucken heads, for booking my shows, for believing in me and for being such incredible managers, agents and solid mates.

Jules, my squeeze, you are just the fucken best person on earth and that's that. I can prove it! Your never-ending love and tenderness for my wobbly, annoying heart and brain has been the most incredibly touching display of support. May this hangout never end. Thanks for sticking by me.

And oi, you! The legend reading this – thanks, friend. You're the reason, after all, that any of this happens. You're the reason that my actual grown-up job is to create awesome stuff. You've saved me from having to do awful shit like wear a suit and door knock trying to sell people cable television they clearly don't want, goddamnit. I fucking hated that gig and sucked real bad at it. Thanks for the escape key.

Thanks for your support. You're beautiful, bloody champions the lot of ya's.

EBURY PRESS

UK | USA | Canada | Ireland | Australia
India | New Zealand | South Africa | China

Ebury Press is part of the Penguin Random House group of companies whose
addresses can be found at global.penguinrandomhouse.com.

First published by Ebury Press, 2023

Cover photography of Nat by Penguin Random House Australia Pty Ltd

Cover and internal images: retrofuturistic font by shutterstock.com/cybermagician; retro future triangle
graphic by shutterstock.com/Art and Roam; stylised Atari typeface by shutterstock.com/passion artist;
audio cassettes by shutterstock.com/ulrich22, shutterstock.com/dubassy, shutterstock.com/ESB Professional
and shutterstock.com/Martin Bergsma; portable compact disc player by shutterstock.com/maramade;
vinyl record by shutterstock.com/Serg001; cassette tapes in a dish by Adobe Stock/sorayut; vinyl record
with knife and fork by Adobe Stock/digiselector; doughnut cookie headset by Adobe Stock/deagreez.

Cover, text design and typesetting by Adam Laszczuk © Penguin Random House Australia

Design and illustrations pp 12–13, 338–339 & 384–385 by Nat's What I Reckon

Printed and bound in China

A catalogue record for this
book is available from the
National Library of Australia

NATIONAL
LIBRARY
OF AUSTRALIA

ISBN 978 1 76134 386 5

penguin.com.au

*We at Penguin Random House Australia acknowledge that Aboriginal and Torres Strait Islander
peoples are the first storytellers and Traditional Custodians of the land on which we live and work.
We honour Aboriginal and Torres Strait Islander peoples' continuous connection to Country, waters,
skies and communities. We celebrate Aboriginal and Torres Strait Islander stories, traditions and
living cultures; and we pay our respects to Elders past and present.*

CONTRIBUTORS

JULIA GEE

Jules is Nat's creative co-conspirator, life accomplice and background cackle on Nat's What I Reckon. A graphic designer by trade, Jules spent over fifteen years in the magazine publishing industry and events industries before joining Nat full time. In her previous life she worked for titles such as *New Scientist*, *Indesign*, *Habitus*, *B&T* and *Architecture & Design*, as well as Cancer Council NSW. When she's not working on artwork for the channel, she can often be found indulging her love of cheese and *RuPaul's Drag Race*, cuddling her house chickens (ragdoll cats), dancing (badly), gaming (also badly) or playing drums. Follow her behind-the-scenes adventures at 🔘 @holy_bat_syllables and her art at 🔘 @housechickenstudios.

BUNKWAA

Bunkwaa is an Australian comic book artist, animator and illustrator. His art is a sleight-of-hand journey into hyper-cartoon worlds, a kaleidoscopic ride full of characters, worlds within worlds and faces within faces. You can connect with him at 🔘 @bunkwaa and learn more about his latest projects at **bunkwaa.com**.

GLENN 'GLENNO' SMITH

Glenno is a desk-bound art tradesman who feels both lucky to draw stuff for a living as well as driven nuts by the stuff he is asked to draw. (His fault for living in the most stupidly expensive place on earth and working with rock 'n' roll types.) His overachievements can be seen via 🔘 @glennoart and at **glennoart.com**.

His amazing and beautiful wife is Gina, his weird cats are Roppongi, Panchetta and Koenji Greyjoy, and his bands are Chinese Burns Unit, Hellebores and Outcest.

ONNIE O'LEARY

Onnie O'Leary has been tattooing since 2011 after achieving a Bachelor of Visual Arts from Sydney College of the Arts in 2008. While her practice encompasses tattooing, print making, drawing, design and illustration, her focus is on graphic and brightly coloured pin-up style artwork, using geometric shapes to frame her work and eye-catching colour fades with a focus on traditional tattoo techniques to make these designs stand the test of time. Inspired by the erotic comic book styles of European artists in the 70s and 80s, she creates unique tattoos for clients both local and international. Onnie has been working at TLD Tattoo since 2017, and hopes to for many years to come. 🔘 @onnieolearytattoo

WARRICK McMILES

Warrick McMiles is a proud Kamilaroi man, Australian artist, illustrator and tattooist based in Sydney's Inner West. From drawing his favourite cartoons as a kid, to graffiti as a teen, to being commissioned to produce murals all across Sydney, his influences include his world travels in the Royal Australian Navy, 80s and 90s pop culture and the street art and hip-hop scenes. You can find Warrick at the Something Original tattoo studio in Newtown, Sydney, Gadigal Country, and at 🔘 @warrick_mcmiles.